SPRINGING *Forth*

Growing Younger while Older

Flora L. Williams,
Ph.D., M.Div., R.F.C.

WESTBOW
PRESS®
A DIVISION OF THOMAS NELSON
& ZONDERVAN

Copyright © 2016 Flora L. Williams, Ph.D., M.Div., R.F.C.

All rights reserved. No part of this book may be used or reproduced by any means, graphic, electronic, or mechanical, including photocopying, recording, taping or by any information storage retrieval system without the written permission of the author except in the case of brief quotations embodied in critical articles and reviews.

WestBow Press books may be ordered through booksellers or by contacting:

WestBow Press
A Division of Thomas Nelson & Zondervan
1663 Liberty Drive
Bloomington, IN 47403
www.westbowpress.com
1 (866) 928-1240

Because of the dynamic nature of the Internet, any web addresses or links contained in this book may have changed since publication and may no longer be valid. The views expressed in this work are solely those of the author and do not necessarily reflect the views of the publisher, and the publisher hereby disclaims any responsibility for them.

Any people depicted in stock imagery provided by Thinkstock are models, and such images are being used for illustrative purposes only.
Certain stock imagery © Thinkstock.

ISBN: 978-1-5127-1724-2 (sc)
ISBN: 978-1-5127-1725-9 (e)

Library of Congress Control Number: 2015919479

Print information available on the last page.

WestBow Press rev. date: 4/11/2016

Springing Forth is dedicated to God, who calls me to write and gives me the words and energy to type. Also, *Springing Forth* is dedicated to my husband, Leiw, who is with me along the way. I also dedicate this work to the people who report that the information in *Springing Forth* has changed their lives and renewed their hope.

About the Author

Rev. Dr. Flora L. Williams is a professor emerita from Purdue University, an ordained minister of the Church of the Brethren, a church musician, a writer, a speaker, a registered financial consultant (retired), a mother of three children, and a grandmother of four grandchildren. Her faith journey is the most important venture for her and teaches her through life trials, painful and peaceful. She credits any accomplishments to the leading and energizing of the Holy Spirit. Her motto is "Glorify God and serve others." She exemplifies how the Holy Spirit moves ordinary people to do extraordinary things.

Her early years were filled with music contests, becoming first clarinetist, attending Camp Mack, starting a peace fellowship, and becoming a high school valedictorian in Lakeville, Indiana. Her educational journey continued at Manchester College, where she majored in music and education, receiving a bachelor of science degree. She earned her master's and PhD degrees from Purdue University, and in 2006, a master of divinity degree from Bethany Theological Seminary. Her working career included eight years in the public schools; thirty-two years at Purdue University teaching financial counseling and planning, family economics, and family resource management; one year teaching at the University of California at Davis; six weeks at Jiao Tong University in Shanghai, China; and six months at Viscosa Federal University in Brazil, where she initiated the graduate program. As a full professor, she directed twenty-three graduate students' research and taught graduate and undergraduate courses.

Her writing journey includes nineteen books on family economics, credit, and financial counseling as well as three inspirational books: *Hand in Hand with God*; *Renewal: Flora's Poetry*; and one book that combines the spiritual and the factual—*The Shepherd's Guide through the Valley of Debt and Financial Change* is a comprehensive manual on financial management, counseling, and spiritual guidance. She wrote more than one hundred research articles and papers on resource management, quality of life, family financial expenditures, poverty, financial counseling, and public policy impacts. These were presented in countries around the world and in the United States.

She founded and then directed a financial advising clinic for twenty-five years. It was a teaching clinic, and it was awarded with the designation of outstanding financial counseling center in the United States in 2001.

She developed texts and testing for certification for the National Foundation for Consumer Credit. She was for many years an accredited financial counselor.

Her professional journey has included conducting workshops; training union counselors; speaking at plant closings; serving as an economic expert on family services in courts; being keynote speaker at caregiver and disability meetings and professional conferences; reviewing papers; and working on boards of directors or trustees for InCharge Institute, Consumer Credit Counseling, and International Quality of Life Research.

Her received awards and professional recognitions are

numerous, including the Sagamore of the Wabash (the highest Indiana award given); the Golden Medallion for scholarship and encouraging women faculty and students; Purdue University and Manchester College outstanding alumna awards; the Labor Union Counseling Award; a Consumer Credit Counseling Service contribution award; a listing in *Who's Who of America*; and membership in the International Society of Poetry. She is past president and vice-president of the international Association for Financial Counseling and Planning Education (AFCPE). By that organization she was awarded the designation of "fellow." Now she is a registered financial consultant.

She speaks at national conventions, university organizations, churches, community groups, and groups with disabilities.

She was in-training and interim pastor at Christ Our Shepherd church in Greenwood, Indiana. She was a chaplain intern at Indiana University Medical Center, Riley Children's Hospital, and the Brethren Home in Greenville, Ohio.

She and her husband give worship services and memorials at assisted living homes and retirement communities. Programs include musical presentations with singing and playing—with one hand—the piano, keyboard, and organ.

Her hobbies include music, gardening, and writing poetry to praise God.

Contents

Part 1: Steps, Scripture, and Song

Step 1: Cry and Confess for Reconciliation and Repair..........1

Step 2: Burn the Trash, the Ugly, and the Painful Past..........6

Step 3: Have a Funeral for Parts of Your Past Life..........10

Step 4: Sweep and Clean the Rooms of Your Heart for Refilling..........14

Step 5: Take Authority over Satan and Demons, Not Being Controlled by Them..........17

Step 6: Pray Without Ceasing..........24

Step 7: Pray for the Holy Spirit to Come into Your Life..........31

Step 8: Change for Renewing Daily..........39

Step 9:   For Opening Possibilities, Be Better, Not Bitter. 45

Step 10: Praise to Open a Window for God's Healing 50

Step 11: Be Grateful to Drive Out Depression 54

Step 12: Handle Worries and Be Yoked to the Lord, Who Carries Your Burdens 57

Step 13: Handle Fear and Improve Faith 64

Step 14: Be Productive—Keep Going But Also Keep Serving 68

Step 15: Associate with Godly, Positive People for Progress 73

Step 16: Handle Anger So It Will Not Choke You 78

Step 17: Change Scenery—Visible and Invisible 86

Step 18: Do Acts of Kindness 90

Step 19: Lift Loneliness to the Light 94

Step 20: Breathe for Healing of Body and Renewing of Spirit 101

Step 21: Accept the New Normal for Renewing Life 105

Step 22: Stand on the Promises for Strength. .111

Step 23: Change Your Reference Group and Gain a New Identity.................119

Step 24: Use Light for Daily Guidance...... 122

Step 25: Use Water for Purifying and Satisfying...................... 128

Step 26: Grow with Suffering............... 132

Step 27: See Signs and Wonders; Have Visions and Dreams............... 138

Step 28: Sing, Whistle, Play an Instrument, or Hum in Concert with the Spirit (Outwardly or Inwardly) 143

Step 29: Share Wisdom, Skills, Experience, and Love 147

Step 30: Look Up; Look Forward; Look Inward to Your Beautiful Self Who Has Survived and Overcome Obstacles; Look to God and to the Place God Has Prepared for You ... 152

Part 2: Enlightenment, Edification, and Education

Grief in Seniors........................... 162

Grief after Long Caregiving 172

Medicine Management..................... 179

Traveling............................ 183
My Spiritual Journey.................. 188
Preparing for Death with Legal and Financial Issues................................ 197
Our Sister Jean 202
Facing Death: Reflections on the Process.... 205
Caregiving Challenge and Charm 229
Beyond the Back Scratcher 232
Arise from Addictions.................... 243
Abuse of Vulnerable Adults: Alleviate It with Courage 261

Part 3: Prayer, Praise, and Power

Life Renewal 279
My Heart............................ 281
I Lost a Part of Me 283
Too Busy to Care 288
You Are All Right.................... 290
Pain................................ 292
Gratitude to Drive the Demons Away 295
Thanks Giving Every Day 297
Wake Up............................ 299
Weak Knees 300
Garden for My Soul 301

Just a Little Son Light 302

Lesson of the Falling Leaves 304

Jesus, O Rescue Us 306

If We Lose All 307

After Hope Is Gone 308

Savior of Suffering 310

Living with Chronics 313

Silent Prayer 316

Cleaning House 320

Walking with Jesus 322

Moving Along—The New Year 324

Lead Me to Victory 326

A Moment in Eternity 328

Conclusion: The Key to Continued Renewal 330

Introduction

We all experience loss, suffering, pain, disappointment, loneliness, and the necessity to change environments or groups at some time of our lives. This book gives concrete and inspiring ways to become renewed, stronger, healed, and hopeful.

I was a full professor at a major university, doing research, teaching, and traveling at various places in the world. But on one trip I was injured in a tragic accident when riding in a tour van in Mexico. I chose this for opportunity, not disaster.

The theme for the entire book is based on this message from the Bible:

> So we do not lose heart. Even though our outer nature is wasting away, our inner nature is being renewed day by

day. For this slight momentarily affliction is preparing us for an eternal weight of glory beyond all measure, because we look not at what can be seen but what cannot be seen; for what can be seen is temporary, but what cannot be seen is eternal. (2 Corinthians 4:16–18 *NRSV*)[1]

We can increase our understanding of this group of verses from Corinthians by examining four additional translations of the Bible and finding the most meaningful words for us.

- *New Living Translation.* "That is why we never give up. Though our bodies are dying, our spirits are being renewed every day. For our present troubles are small and won't last very long. Yet they produce for us a glory that vastly outweighs them and will last forever! So we don't

---

[1] The *New Revised Standard Version* of the Bible is cited here. Other Scripture quotations in this book are from the *New International Version* (*NIV*) of the Bible unless another translation is noted.

Springing Forth • xiii

look at the troubles we can see now; rather, we fix our gaze on things that cannot be seen. For the things we see now will soon be gone, but the things we cannot see will last forever."

- *Common English Bible.* "So we aren't depressed. But even if our bodies are breaking down on the outside, the person that we are on the inside is being renewed every day. Our temporary minor problems are producing an eternal stockpile of glory for us that are beyond comparison. We don't focus on things that can be seen but on things that can't be seen. The things that can be seen don't last, but the things that can't be seen are eternal."

- *Good News Translation.* "For this reason we never become discouraged. Even though our physical being is gradually decaying, yet our spiritual being is renewed day after day. And this small and temporary trouble we suffer will bring us a tremendous and eternal glory, much greater than the trouble. For we fix our attention, not on things that are seen, but on things that are unseen. What can be seen lasts only for a time, but what cannot be seen lasts forever."

- *The Message (a paraphrase of the Bible).* "So we're not giving up. How could we! Even though on the outside it often looks like things are falling apart on us, on the inside, where God is making new life, not a day goes by without his unfolding grace. These hard times are small potatoes compared to the coming good times, the lavish celebration prepared for us. There's far more here than meets the eye. The things we see now are here today, gone tomorrow. But the things we can't see now will last forever."

A unique contribution of this book is the presentation of the outcome of a search of the Scriptures revealing how older people coped with affliction and how they contributed wisdom. A secondary theme of the book, interwoven throughout, is what the Scriptures say about afflictions and aging.

Afflictions include suffering that is emotional, physical, or spiritual. Afflictions are losses of any type, such as losing employment, family members, friends, wealth, health, bodily parts, educational pursuits, and purpose in life. Afflictions are persecution, damaging prejudices, and demons.

We create a renewed spirit, renewed purpose, and healing with positive steps day by day. The spiritual overrides our physical. Mental activities override the physical. Mind is over matter. We grow spiritually—in spite of our frail or failing bodies—by practices and prayer. We can select those new steps, in addition to the ones we already do, to spring forth.

New life can spring forth every day. Strength for today and hope for tomorrow give power to persevere, ability to contribute, and peace. Changes in our self-identity, attitude, focus, discipline, Scripture reading, and activities renew us. Joy and production continue even with trials, tribulations, and deteriorating health. We can be healed, even if we are not cured. Songs and simple reminders can transform us. Visions can help us to handle identity crises and restore our soul, even when our bodies are failing or confusion surrounds us.

Scriptures support the steps that guide us as to the ways we can have life and have it more abundantly. The concept of steps is in Proverbs 14:15. It says, "The simple believe anything, but the prudent give thought to their *steps*." Further, Proverbs 16:9 says, "In his heart a man plans his course, but the Lord determines his *steps*." A promise is given in Isaiah 42:16: "I will lead the blind by ways they have not known, along unfamiliar paths I will guide them; I will turn the darkness into light before them and make the rough places smooth. And Creator God states, in Isaiah 48:17, "This is what the Lord says—your Redeemer, 'I am the Lord your God, who teaches you what is best for you, who directs you in the way you should go.'"

The thirty steps—specific actions and activities—provide strength in our daily lives for springing forth, renewal, healing, and hope. Scriptures and songs contribute to these steps for our strength, courage, and wisdom. They provide depth for the steps.

Real people have written essays that present reality and give instructions. The contributed articles and my articles cover topics ranging from dealing with grief to traveling well as we age. Most of the essays present technical ways to change as well as inspiration from those who have changed and recovered from afflictions. The essays contribute enlightenment, edification, and education.

Reading strong poems give renewal and healing in the face of loss, suffering, and aging. The poems continue the themes in the book and contribute to our changing emotionally and spiritually. The poems offer prayers, praise, and power unique to each person's situation.

Part I
Steps, Scripture, and Song

Practical, spiritual, and life-changing steps can renew us daily as we practice them for daily exercises. Scriptures, songs, and poems equip us for this exciting journey.

Part 1
Steps, Scripture and Song

Practical, spiritual, and life-changing steps can renew our lives as we practice them for daily exercise. Scripture, songs, and poems equip us for this exciting journey.

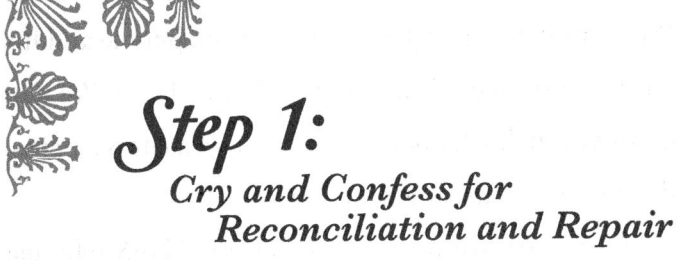

Step 1:
Cry and Confess for Reconciliation and Repair

Cry ... Grieve ... When terrible things happen now or occurred in the distant past, we can become healed by verbalizing them and crying. We read this in Psalm 34:17–18: "The righteous cry out, and the Lord hears them; he delivers them from all their troubles. The Lord is close to the brokenhearted and saves those who are crushed in spirit."

A song entitled "Give Them All to Jesus and He Will Turn Your Sorrow into Joy"[2] asks, "Are you tired of chasing pretty rainbows? Are you tired of spinning round and round? Wrap all the shattered dreams of your life, and at the feet of Jesus, lay them down."

---

[2] Phil Johnson and Bob Benson Sr., "Give Them All to Jesus and He Will Turn Your Sorrow into Joy," in *Lift Him Up* (Benson Co.). Copyright © 1975 Dimension Music. International copyright secured. Capitolcmglicensing.com. All rights reserved.

It is okay to cry. Let it all out. Crying reduces stress. It is our safety valve. Jesus cried for the people and his friend who died. "Jesus wept" (John 11:35). We can confess our hurts, pain, mistakes, weaknesses, sins, disappointments, anger, and grief.

Our tears are not in vain. Psalm 126:5 tells us: "Those who sow with tears will reap with songs of joy." In 2 Kings 20:5, the Bible tells us that God pays attention when we express our suffering: "Go back and tell Hezekiah, the ruler of my people. 'This is what the LORD, the God of your father David, says: I have heard your prayer and seen your tears; I will heal you. On the third day from now you will go up to the temple of the LORD.'"

Here are other relevant Scriptures:

- Lamentations 1:16: "This is why I weep and my eyes overflow with tears. No one is near to comfort me. No one to restore my spirit. My children are destitute because the enemy has prevailed."

- 2 Corinthians 2:4: "For I wrote you out of great distress and anguish of heart and with many tears, not to grieve you but to let you know the depth of my love for you."

- Hebrews 5:7: "During the days of Jesus' life on earth, he offered up prayers and petitions with fervent cries and tears to the one who could save him from death, and he was heard because of his reverent submission."

- Isaiah 65:17–19 (*New King James Version*): "For behold, I create new heavens and a new earth; and the former shall not be remembered or come to mind … I will rejoice in Jerusalem, and joy in my people. The voice of weeping shall no longer be heard in her, nor the voice of crying."

Our first daily renewal, then, is asking for forgiveness, repenting (turning, changing), and confessing. Remember no sin is too great for God to forgive. These open us for possibilities of renewal. We can thank God for His forgiveness. This can be a prayer. A powerful verse is Ezekiel 18:31–32 (*NRSV*): "Cast away from you all the transgressions that you have committed against me, and get yourself a new heart and a new spirit! Why will you die, …? For I have no pleasure in the death of anyone, says the Lord God. Turn, then, and live!"

Forgiveness is a part of the crying process. We are forgiven as we forgive others. It is hard to forgive sometimes. Ability to forgive is a gift from the Holy Spirit. Some find writing a letter, even posthumously, is helpful in asking forgiveness. Each of us can now write things we have always wanted to say to someone and mail them. We can write these things even after he or she has died.

An old song can give new hope: "Out of the Depths I Cry to You."[3] "Out of the depths I cry to you; O Lord now hear me calling. Incline your ear to my distress in spite of my rebelling. Do not regard my sinful deeds. Send me the grace my spirit needs; without it I am nothing." Another prayer song is "Hear My Cry,"[4] based on Psalm 61:1: "Hear my cry, O Lord, attend

---

[3] Martin Luther, "Out of the Depths I Cry to You" (1523–24), based on Psalm 130, in *Etlich Christlich Lieder* (1524); trans. Gracia Grindal, *Lutheran Book of Worship* (1978); alt. translation copyright © 1978 *Lutheran Book of Worship*.

[4] Lyricist and composer unknown. In *Maranatha! Music*, copyright © 1990.

unto my prayer; From the end of the earth will I cry unto Thee. And when my heart is overwhelmed, Please lead me to the Rock that is higher than I, that is higher than I."

I rejoice; God is with me in turning sorrow into joy.

We can receive healing when we "Cry out 'Save us, O God our Savior; gather us and deliver us from the nations, that we may give thanks to your holy name, that we may glory in your praise'" (1 Chronicles 16:35).

The hope is in Psalm 142:1–3: "I cry aloud to the Lord; I lift up my voice to the Lord for mercy. I pour out my complaint before him; before I tell him my trouble. When my spirit grows faint within me, it is you who knows my way."

We step from the past and leave injuries, sorrows, mistakes, disappointments, and guilt. We seek new paths and purposes. The Spirit leads us. "All this is from God, who reconciled us to himself through Christ and gave us the ministry of reconciliation" (2 Corinthians 4:18) "with joy in your presence, with eternal pleasures at your right hand" (Psalm 16:11).

Step 2:
Burn the Trash, the Ugly, and the Painful Past

What do you want gone from your life? Write it on a piece of paper and burn it. As the smoke goes up, new beginnings and new hope emerge. Abandon the old life for a new chapter, with new changes, new goals, and new roles. Retain the memories that uplift you and give you alertness and courage. Discard the harmful, bitter, and painful ones. Burn the abuses, curses, hurts, mistakes, and badness that haunt us.

Different types of loss can involve varying times for us to mourn, reflect, and gain renewal. For some losses it takes fifteen minutes and for others fifteen days, fifteen months, or fifteen years.

The discipline can be to consciously "throw out the trash," emotionally and socially. This can be a daily or weekly practice. When we throw out the material garbage, dirt, and clutter to the bin each day or week, we can remind ourselves of the daily step for internal and social cleansing and renewal.

The burning associated with sacrifices in the Old Testament was applied to valuable and good things. In our case, destroying the negative things and memories in our lives assists in healing. By means of fire, spiritual renewal experiences result, as described in Leviticus 2:9: "The priest shall remove from the grain offering its token portion and turn this into smoke on the altar, an offering by fire of pleasing odor to the Lord." Also, Leviticus 5:12 says, "You shall bring it to the priest, and the priest shall scoop up a handful of it as its memorial portion, and turn this into smoke on the altar, with the offerings by fire to the Lord; it is a sin offering. (*NRSV* is used throughout Step 2.)

Destroying the negative by fire in the New Testament is described in Matthew 7:19: "Every tree that does not bear good fruit is cut down and thrown into the fire." Also, Matthew 13:40 says, "Just as the weeds are collected and burned up with fire, so will it be at the end of the age."

Relevant to our renewal is the promise delivered by John the Baptist in Matthew 3:11: "I baptize you with water for repentance, but one who is more powerful than I is coming after me; I am not worthy to carry his sandals. He will baptize you with the *Holy Spirit and fire*" (emphasis mine).

Start a new chapter. Be renewed by visualizing—turning the page to a new chapter in your life rather than being controlled by the past. We have to improve self-esteem. First we need to realize that we are created in the image of God with a certain value and purpose in our life. Then we can set new goals and have new roles. We can embrace new opportunities. Have new purposes for living. Learn new skills. Be patient. Pray, persevere, practice, and proceed with power. Rejoice in feeling progress, not perfection.

When there is a loss of spouse, job, or educational pursuit, consider it an opportunity for a new chapter. Tell yourself, "Every day is a new day, a new chance." But on some days our steps are like climbing up a sand dune—we take two steps forward and one backward. The progress depends on determination and focus, although we have setbacks. Sometimes we trip, fall, or slide completely to the bottom. Then we must start over again. The body is sometimes weak, but strength of purpose through the Spirit can help us climb to the top. We can walk and rejoice because God is with us through the Spirit who renews us!

We move forward after cleansing by singing the song "This Is a Day of New Beginnings."[5]

> [third verse] Then let us, with the Spirit's daring, step from the past and leave behind our disappointment, guilt, and grieving, seeking new paths, and sure to find.

> [fourth verse] Christ is alive, and goes before us to show and share what love can do. This is a day of new beginnings—our God is making all things new.

---

[5] Brian Wren, "This Is a Day of New Beginnings" (1978), in *Faith Looking Forward*. Copyright © 1983, 1987 Hope Publishing Co., Carol Stream, IL 60188. All rights reserved. Used by permission.

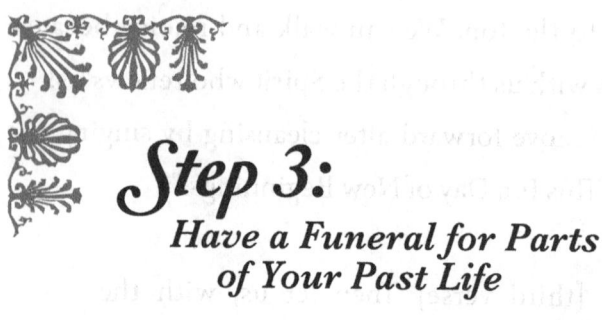

Step 3:
Have a Funeral for Parts of Your Past Life

We can have a formal ceremony, with ritual, written by ourselves, to help come to a final closure of anything that binds or hinders our race toward what God has for us. Consider losses as opportunities for new beginnings. We can "die with Christ, rise with Christ." This is explained in Colossians 2:12–13: "When you were buried with Him in baptism, you were also raised with him through faith in the power of God ... And when you were dead in trespasses, God made you alive together with Him, when he forgave us all our trespasses, erasing the record that stood against us with its legal demands. He set this aside, nailing it to the cross." (*NRSV* is used throughout Step 3.)

The concept of being buried and raised for healing and renewal is described in Romans 6:4: "Therefore we have been buried with him in baptism into death, so that, just as Christ was raised from the dead by the glory of the Father, so we might walk in newness of life."

Jesus died for us so that we can be freed from the burden of sin, transgressions, and our wrongs. Then we can freely know the love of God. Jesus suffered and died and afterward rose victoriously. Jesus conquered death. Recall that Jesus arose so that we can know the power of the resurrection.

Today, here and now, we can be resurrected to a new, joyous life—life in its fullness. When evil or disturbing thoughts come to roost on us, we can shout "Resurrection!" But in order to rise with Christ, first we must die with Christ. We have to die to our sins, mistakes, terrors, fears, torments, mistakes, and addictions.

Die to these. Put aside or bury regrets, hurtful things, bad habits, sins of commission and omission, social injustice sins, guilt, shame, remorse, terrors, torments, brokenness, evil spirits, filth, blows and knockdowns, the pain of losses, and feelings of inadequacy.

Accept that we are forgiven—moving forth with Jesus walking beside us, in us, arising each day with us, with mercies new every morning, and with the Spirit filling us with power. To feel the love of God brings peace and the joy of new life.

"God so loved the world that He sent his only son that whosoever believeth in Him will not perish but have everlasting life" (John 3:16). God does not want us to perish in our problems, troubles, and tragedies; He does want us to accept His love and have an everlasting, joyous, and abundant life. We can choose to remain in our predicaments and perish, or we can choose life after burying the past! Sometimes we have to make a clean break with the past to make a fresh new beginning. We can continuously be cleansed daily.

A promise is in Ephesians 4:20–24: "You were taught to put away your former way of life, your old self, corrupt and deluded by lusts, and to be renewed in the spirit of your minds, and to clothe yourself with new self, created according to the likeness of God in true righteousness and holiness."

When death of the past or a funeral occurs, we can sing "When Grief Is Raw."[6] "When grief is raw and music goes unheard and thought is numb, we have no

---

[6] Brian Wren, "When Grief Is Raw," published in *Faith Looking Forward*. Copyright © 1983 Hope Publishing Co., Carol Stream, IL 60188. All rights reserved. Used by permission.

polished phrases to recite. You are our Lord. In faith we grasp familiar words: 'I am the resurrection, I am life."

We rise and rejoice as the song "You Raise Me Up" conveys:[7] "You raise me up, so I can stand on mountains; You raise me up to walk on stormy seas; I am strong when I am on your shoulders; You raise me up to be more than I can be."

So, we rejoice. God is with us and helps us rise, daily. The evidence of success is getting up when we fall. Proverbs 24:16 says: "For though a righteous man [woman] falls seven times, he [she] rises again."

---

[7] Rolf Lovland and Brendan Graham, "You Raise Me Up," Copyright © 2002 Matt Music, Peermusic (UK) Ltd., Curb Songs, Universal Music Publishing AB, Peermusic (Ireland) Ltd., WB Music Corp.

Step 4:
Sweep and Clean the Rooms of Your Heart for Refilling

It is time to sweep every corner of our hearts of evil and negative thoughts, hidden bitterness, repressed lies, poisons, vices, and foolish desires. We need a spring cleaning to spring forth in new life. It includes scrubbing, vacuuming, blowing out, removing spots and stains.

Cleaning makes room for the Spirit to come in with new thoughts, habits, interests, and feelings. One new aim is to love every person, every day, wherever we meet on the way. We express love by bestowing kindnesses, loving, complimenting, encouraging, and similar actions.

Scripture, however, adds a warning about this analogy to house cleaning. Severe consequences can occur if the cleaning is not followed by continued renewal. The warning is in Matthew 12:43–45: "When an impure spirit comes out of a person, it goes through arid places seeking rest and does not find it. Then it says, 'I will return to the house I left.' When it arrives, it finds the house unoccupied, swept clean and put in order. Then it goes and takes with it seven other spirits more wicked than itself, and they go in and live there. And the final condition of that person is worse than the first. That is how it will be with this wicked generation."

A prayer song is "Search Me, O God (or Cleanse Me)"[8]:

> Search me, O God, and know my heart today. Try me, O Savior, know my thoughts, I pray; See if there be some wicked way in me; Cleanse me from every sin, and set me free.

Psychology principles also imply that new goals or habits are necessary to replace old goals or bad habits. Cleaning and replacing goes only so far if not directed by the Lord. After confessing (cleaning) we can pray, "God, since you know our needs for refurbishing better than we do, supply us wholesale for our whole self."

---

[8] James E. Orr, "Search Me, O God (or Cleanse Me)" (1936), based on Psalm 51:1–2. Public Domain.

We overcome barriers and refill our hearts by concentrating on the delights God has provided, such as flowers, trees, rocks, birds, butterflies, pleasant people, grandchildren, collections, music, volunteering, sports, and hobbies. Following the thirty good steps in this book helps overcome barriers and ways to refill our hearts and minds..

We move forward after cleansing by singing the song "This Is a Day of New Beginnings."[9]

> This is a day of new beginnings,
> Time to remember and move on,
> Time to believe what love is bringing,
> Laying to rest the pain that's gone.
>
> For by the life and death of Jesus,
> God's mighty Spirit, now and then,
> Can make for us a world of difference,
> As faith and hope are born again.

Rejoice!

---

[9] Brian Wren, "This Is a Day of New Beginnings" (1978), in *Faith Looking Forward.* Copyright © 1983, 1987 Hope Publishing Co., Carol Stream, IL 60188. All rights reserved. Used by permission.

Step 5:
Take Authority over Satan and Demons, Not Being Controlled by Them

Satan and demons are barriers to becoming healed and renewed. We cannot take lightly the power of the demonic. Demons are mentioned eighty-four times in the Scripture. In Matthew 4:24 we read of actions of Jesus regarding demons: "News about him spread all over Syria, and people brought to him all who were ill with various diseases, those suffering severe pain, the demon-possessed, those having seizures, and the paralyzed; and he healed them." Another example is in Matthew 8:16: "When evening came, many who were demon-possessed were brought to him, and he drove out the spirits with a word and healed all the sick."

We must resist Satan and have authority in the power of Christ. To quote 1 Corinthians 10:21: "You cannot drink the cup of the Lord and the cup of demons too; you cannot have a part in both the Lord's Table and the table of demons."

It is sad when people do not know how to recognize Satan and destroy his influence in their lives. Satan is deceptive, is the author of lies, and is described as an angel of light. He is surrounded by darkness and dark people. He has power, and his beings, games, and statues have power over our lives when we give him authority and yield to his powerful influences.

We can say, "Get behind me Satan and don't push"; "In the name of Jesus, go!" We can shout, "Freedom in the name of Jesus!" We can read the story of Job in the Old Testament for more instructions.

Zechariah 3:2 says, "The LORD said to Satan, 'The Lord rebuke YOU, Satan! The LORD, who has chosen Jerusalem, rebuke you! Is not this man a burning stick snatched from the fire?'" In Matthew 4:10 we read: "Jesus said to him, 'Away from me, Satan! For it is written: 'Worship the Lord your God, and serve him only.'"

Other instructions and examples are in relevant biblical texts:

- Mark 4:15: "Some people are like seed along the path, where the word is sown. As soon as they hear it, Satan comes and takes away the word that was sown in them."

- Mark 8:33: "Then Jesus turned and looked at his disciples and rebuked Peter. 'Get behind me, Satan!' he said. 'You do not have in mind the concerns of God, but merely human concerns.'" (See Matthew 16:23.)

- 1 Corinthians 7:5: "Do not deprive each other except perhaps by mutual consent and for a time, so that you may devote yourselves to prayer. Then come together again so that Satan will not tempt you because of your lack of self-control."

- 2 Corinthians 2:10–11: "Anyone you forgive, I also forgive. And what I have forgiven—if there was anything to forgive—I have forgiven in the sight of Christ for your sake, in order that Satan might not outwit us. For we are not unaware of his schemes."

Jesus said we can do greater things than He did when we are filled with the Holy Spirit. Here is how He had authority over real demon influences. Matthew 10:8 tells us that Jesus said, "Heal the sick, raise the dead, cleanse those who have leprosy, drive out demons. Freely you have received; freely give." Further, Jesus said in Matthew 12:28: "But if it is by the Spirit of God that I drive out demons, then the kingdom of God has come upon you." In Matthew 17:18 we read: "Jesus rebuked the demon, and it came out of the boy, and he was healed at that moment." And Luke 9:1 states: "When Jesus had called the Twelve together, he gave them power and authority to drive out all demons and to cure diseases."

The greatest promise God gives us in the Bible is in Romans 8:38–39: "For I am convinced that neither death nor life, neither angels nor demons, neither the present nor the future, nor any powers, neither height nor depth, nor anything else in all creation, will be able to separate us from the love of God that is in Christ Jesus our Lord."

Steps to take authority over Satan include the following:

1. Keep a holy home, which includes watching out for DVDs, television shows, card games, and other things people may bring to your home. Some hold demonic programming. Scripture warns us to be cautious about what we see, hear, and allow into our hearts. Be careful of the music we listen to. Music can either be soothing and calming or divisive; spiritual or carnal.

2. Feed the Holy Spirit and not the spirit of the world.

3. Be holy yourself. We cannot combat Satan when we are carnal. Be alert. Satan and demons come all the time. In 1 Corinthians 2:12, the Bible says, "Now we have received not the spirit of the world, but the Spirit that is from God, so that we may understand the gifts bestowed on us by God."

4. Respond with the authority of the Word of God and the living presence of Jesus. Satan has no choice but to respond to this authority.

Our opinions do not matter. (See Revelations 12:7-17, 20:1-3, 10)

5. Use an experienced pastor or person who is experienced to assist in removing Satan, demons, and their influence. However, if our house and heart are not cleansed and refilled, Satan and demons will return.

6. Read a Scripture chapter whenever you are tempted by a bad addiction or tempted to forego something that you have been called by God to do.

Moving on from any demon-related obsessions is important for renewal. Demons can be considered the "D" of disturbances that prevent us from feeling joyful and renewed: disappointments, discouragements, distresses, despair, defeatist attitude, diseases, disability, disturbing aches and pains, and depression.

We can call on the Lord today for control and cure of the D's of demons. Much of the work of Jesus was driving out demons and He is working today, moment by moment. We are to be aware of evil ones and deception. Be shrewd. Do not be taken advantage of, fall for a scam, or be defrauded in time or money. Do not be abused by children or a caregiver. Jesus said in Matthew 10:16, "I am sending you out like sheep among wolves. Therefore be as shrewd as snakes and as innocent as doves." In the story of Jacob and Esau of the Old Testament, the firstborn's "blessing" is given, through deception, to the second born. (See Genesis 27:5–38.)

Currently there is more discussion of the spiritual warfare and attacks upon us. A pertinent song is "Mighty Warrior."[10] "Mighty Warrior, dressed for battle; Holy Lord of all is He. Commander-in-Chief, bring us to attention, Lead us into battle to crush the enemy."

We can pray every day as suggested in the Lord's Prayer: Keep us from the evil one and from evil. We can turn enemies into friends. As Jesus said we can love our enemies and "turn the other cheek." We can put our demons at bay. We have God's power and we can develop the will.

We can rejoice when facing enemies, because God is with us!

---

[10] Debbye Graafsma, "Mighty Warrior," based on Exodus 15:3. Copyright © 1983 Integrity's Hosanna Music.

Step 6:
Pray Without Ceasing

Pray every day in every way. Converse constantly with God. Live on two levels—heaven and earth—all the time. Set a time to pray the Lord's Prayer (Matthew 6:9-13) every day or the rosary, maybe with someone else at a distance. (It includes asking for deliverance from the evil one as mentioned in the Prayer.) As Jesus tells us in Luke 22:19 and 1 Corinthians 11:24, remember Him when we break bread or drink. Rather than saying, "It is time to eat," announce, "It is time to pray and eat."

When a friend reviewed an early draft of this book, she commented, "Prayer is the foundation for the rest of the steps. Without a solid foundation of prayer, the rest will crumble. Prayer brings us closer to God and makes us more able to submit to God's will/purpose and plan. When we can sit quietly and listen for that 'still small voice,' we will gain the insight we need to cope with what is before us. Prayer changes us, rather than convincing God to do as we want."

Prayer includes both talking and listening to God. A scriptural song, based on Isaiah 40:31, is "They That Wait Upon the Lord."[11] "They that wait upon the Lord shall renew their strength. They shall mount up with wings like eagles. They shall run, and not be weary; They shall walk, and not faint. Teach me Lord, teach me Lord to wait."

Prayer makes things possible, overcoming the barriers and the obstacles. Prayer brings possibilities beyond imagination. It brings more happiness than we thought possible. We are told in the Scripture that if we pray in Jesus' name, we will receive the desires of our heart. Pray, as we are reminded in Ephesians 6:18: "And pray in the Spirit on all occasions with all kinds of prayers and requests. With this in mind, be alert and always keep on praying for all the Lord's people."

In John 16:22–24, Jesus says, "So with you: Now is your time of grief, but I will see you again and you will

---

[11] Stuart Hamblen, "They That Wait Upon the Lord," in *Hymnal: A Worship Book* (Elgin, IL: Brethren Press). Copyright © 1992.

rejoice, and no one will take away your joy. In that day you will no longer ask me anything. Very truly I tell you, my Father will give you whatever you ask in my name. Until now you have not asked for anything in my name. Ask and you will receive, and your joy will be complete." Keep praying, asking, seeking, knocking. "The door will be opened for you" (Matthew 7:7).

With prayer, nothing is impossible with God. (See Luke 1:37.) Even with prayer, however, suffering occurs. (Jesus wept over Lazarus's death. Mary suffered with Christ. Disciples were persecuted.) Sometimes our prayers do not seem to be answered. Even with prayer, difficult conditions may continue or get worse. Or nothing happens to change the hearts of others.

How can we handle these contradictions? Why, when we pray and have great faith, does nothing happen or we continue to suffer and have calamities? We wonder if God hears us, and like Jesus on the cross, we ask, "Has God forsaken us?" Sometimes we don't pray for the right thing. We may be too involved with our own will or desires. Sometimes we put a time limit on God's answer. We are not willing to wait. What are the types of answers that God provides to our prayer? Consider the following examples:

1. No—if we do not pray in Jesus' name, His will, His truth, His plan for us.

2. No—if God knows better than we do about what is best for us, what is better happiness, what is ultimate strength and happiness, such as a surgery to get better. (See the story of Stephen in Acts 7:54-66, who, while being stoned to death, looked to heaven and saw Jesus standing at the right hand of God.)

3. No, not yet—because others have free will to choose their actions and need to be open to God's leading, which impact us. We can pray that they are not hard-hearted or controlled by the evil one. (Stephen called them hard-hearted and not listening to the laws the angels told them.).

4. No—because God allows accidents or misery to happen so that His glory will be revealed, so He will be glorified in due time. Stephen was an example, changing lives such as the life of Saul, who became Paul. Today, many Christians try

to imitate Stephen when they are dying from illnesses or persecution.

5. Yes—but the result is different than the change for which we prayed. Good can come from what we considered unanswered prayer, resulting in greater dependence on God, more maturity and perseverance, more understanding, more giving of comfort to others going through pain and trials, and greater learning from mistakes to provide even more future goodness and happiness.

Further suggestions, based on the Scriptures, about praying, include the following:

- First, lift up praise. We have a Creator who cares about us, with wondrous love through which nothing can separate us from Him. We give God praise that we see His hand controlling the world. Praise that the Holy Spirit is "moving in our midst." Praise that God hears us.

- Second, lay down the sins and sorrows at Jesus' feet. Then make requests before our Creator.

Be specific naming the person and the specific condition. An example is my answer to a visiting minister when he asked if I had a prayer request. "Yes," I said, "pray that my sodium level be raised, as it was dangerously low from an accident." It was higher in the morning.

- Third, having presented your requests to God, express to Him your trust in all areas of your life. Accept that God's will be done, not our weak imagination and plans as dominated by worldly passions and idols. Accept that God's will and plan for us is known, as well as the steps that bring benefit. Acknowledge that God enables greater possibilities than we can imagine and has plans for our good, not harm.

- Fourth, lay out our gratitude for everything. Give thanks for everything, even for God allowing us to be a part of the suffering of a suffering God. (Also, see Colossians 1:24.) Thank God that His hand is directing us, moving us, keeping us from being trapped.

- Fifth, listen to the Creator. Prayer is two-way communication. Take time to listen, perhaps writing ideas on paper. If we don't listen, we risk missing God's guidance, peace, and reassurance. We are uncomfortable with waiting and listening, but it is very important in all relationships. Rejoice, for God is listening and talking to us.

Prayer is the mightiest force in our lives since it connects us to God Almighty. Our praises and thanksgiving open our hearts and minds to receive gifts and blessings; crying about our pain and sorrow brings healing; forgiveness restores our relationships; conversation with God brings transformation of our attitudes, direction for actions; and praying spreads love to others.

The formula for success is: Pray, plan, practice, persevere, be patient, be proactive, hear God's perspective, and receive power, physically, mentally, emotionally, and spiritually.

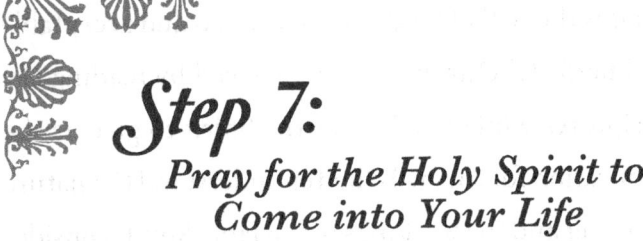

Step 7:
Pray for the Holy Spirit to Come into Your Life

Ordinary people filled with the Spirit can overcome obstacles and be healed. We can pray each day for blessings so that we will be a blessing to others. Jesus told the disciples that they could do greater things than He did, which was healing those everywhere He went. We can pray for healing of ourselves and others.

Prayer is affirming trust. The verse stating that those who "wait upon the Lord will renew their strength" is based on the original word that can be translated either "wait," "hope," or "trust." Some people wait to act until the Spirit fills their soul. Some people report that they wait until the Spirit fills them before getting out of bed.

The renewal message in Romans 12:2 *(NRSV)* is: "Do not be conformed to this world, but be transformed by the renewing of your minds, so that you may discern what is the will of God—what is good and acceptable and perfect." Our minds are renewed by reading the Scriptures while praying for the Spirit to give us the application for them. To better understand the nature of prayer and the workings of the Holy Spirit, consider these Scriptures:

- John 14:15–17: "If you love me, keep my commands. And I will ask the Father, and he will give you another advocate [counselor] to help you and be with you forever—the Spirit of truth. The world cannot accept him, because it neither sees him nor knows him. But you know him, for he lives with you and will be in you."

- John 14:25–27: "All this I have spoken while still with you. But the Advocate, the Holy Spirit, whom the Father will send in my name, will teach you all things and will remind you of everything I have said to you. Peace I leave with you; my peace I give you. I do not give to you as the world gives. Do not let your hearts be troubled and do not be afraid."

Anointing is an outward action or sacrament which involves prayer that invokes the Holy Spirit. Anointing on the forehead with oil in the shape of the cross is useful for infilling of the Holy Spirit. It is an outward sign of an inward change. It can be used for receiving the Holy Spirit, healing, guidance, courage, and peace.

Also, God has anointed persons directly. This is reported in Isaiah 61:1, which says, "The Spirit of the Sovereign LORD is on me because the LORD has anointed me to proclaim good news to the poor. He has sent me to bind up the broken-hearted, to proclaim freedom for the captives and release from darkness for the prisoners."

Wisdom and instructions about anointing are in the following Scriptures:

- Exodus 30:31: "Say to the Israelites, 'This is to be my sacred anointing oil for the generations to come.'"

- Psalm 20:6: "Now this I know: The LORD gives victory to his anointed. He answers him from his heavenly sanctuary with the victorious power of his right hand."

- Psalm 23:5: "You prepare a table before me in the presence of my enemies. You anoint my head with oil; my cup overflows."

- Psalm 28:8: "The LORD is the strength of his people, a fortress of salvation for his anointed one."

- Psalm 45:7: "You love righteousness and hate wickedness; therefore God, your God, has set you above your companions by anointing you with the oil of joy."

- James 5:14: "Is anyone among you sick? Let them call the elders of the church to pray over them and anoint them with oil in the name of the Lord."

- 1 John 2:20: "You have an anointing from the Holy One, and all of you know the truth." (It is a reminder day by day when the oil or memory of the experience is there. One woman had a permanent scar result at the place she was anointed on the forehead.)

- 1 John 2:27: "As for you, the anointing you received from him remains in you, and you do not need anyone to teach you. But as his anointing teaches you about all things and as that anointing is real, not counterfeit—just as it has taught you, remain in him."

- Mark 6:13: "They drove out many demons and anointed many sick people with oil and healed them."

- Hebrews 1:9: "You have loved righteousness and hated wickedness; therefore God, your God, has set you above your companions by anointing you with the oil of joy."

William Gaither explains this step toward renewal in "Come Holy Spirit, We Need Thee."[12]

> Come as a wisdom to children, Come as new sight to the blind, Come, Lord,

---

[12] William Gaither, "Come Holy Spirit, We Need Thee." Copyright © 1964 by William Gaither.

as strength to my weakness, Take me: soul, body and mind.

Another is "Spirit, Now Live in Me."[13]

> O holy dove of God descending, You are the love that knows no ending, All of our shattered dreams You're mending: Spirit, now live in me ... You are the life that starts us growing: Spirit now live in me ... You are that inner voice now calling: Spirit, now live in me ... You are the answer to our yearning: Spirit, now live in me.

Yet another prayer song to the Holy Spirit is "Holy Spirit, Come to Us."[14]

---

[13] Bryan Jeffery Leech, "Spirit, Now Live in Me." Copyright © 1976 Fred Bock Music Co. All rights reserved. Used with permission.

[14] Victoria L. Ullery, "Holy Spirit, Come to Us" (2002), based on Romans 8:26–27. Copyright © 2002 Whotkee R. WeYin Pub. All rights reserved.

> Holy Spirit, come to us. Holy Spirit, pray for us. Holy Spirit, fill our hearts with Your everlasting love.

Sometimes we are too weak or ignorant to know how to pray. We can be comforted by the words in Romans 8:27: "And he who searches our hearts knows the mind of the Spirit, because the Spirit intercedes for God's people in accordance with the will of God."

The step toward renewal is explained in the song "We Do Not Know How to Pray."[15]

> We do not know how to pray, but the Spirit intercedes; all our sighs too deep for words reach the heart of God. We do not know how to pray, but Christ Jesus intercedes; our humanity, in Him, moves the heart of God. We do not know how to pray, but the Spirit knows our needs; all our sorrow, fear,

---

[15] Alan Gaunt, "We Do Not Know How to Pray" (1997), based on Romans 8:26, 33–34. Text copyright © 1997 Stainer & Bell, Ltd. Administered by Hope Publishing Co., Carol Stream, IL 60188. All rights reserved. Used by permission.

and pain wound the heart of God. We do not know how to pray, but as long as Jesus pleads, we shall never be cast out from the heart of God. We do not know how to pray, but Christ's Holy Spirit leads 'till we find creation's peace in the heart of God.

Rejoice! The Holy Spirit is working in us – our hope, our healing, and our power!

I know parents who prayed that their three-year-old would be filled with the Holy Spirit. Later, a professor of spirituality saw her walking, and remarked, "She is filled with the Holy Spirit."

Step 8:
Change for Renewing Daily

To combat the feeling that "all is lost," we can write, on one note card, something that will change. Examples are facing divorce or desertion, change in employment, loss of a friend, illness, or uncompleted educational pursuits. Then write on another card what will not change. Accept the changes and adjust. Learn where other changes can be made. Be creative. Make it an adventure.

"Change is the only evidence of growth" (author unknown). We can pray to have the right words, tone of voice, and attitude. We have to change our purpose in life, our identity, our attitudes, our skills, our physical arrangements, and our prayers. We have to change what we do and how we do it. We can pray daily to know where to change daily. When we have lost something or someone—spouse, child, parent, wealth, employment, mission, educational pursuit, physical ability, or good looks—we have to change. We have to change when we have centered our lives around persons or circumstances which are no longer here. These changes are serious and difficult. They require a time of grieving. Some people take time to lament that they have been left alone. They need discernment, prayer, practice, and perseverance. We can pray for God's wisdom and power to guide us.

The sin is remaining in despair and not embracing changes and doing something to be renewed. Failure to embrace change is a temptation. James said in James 1:13–15,

> When tempted, no one should say, "God is tempting me." For God cannot be tempted by evil, nor does he tempt anyone; but each person is tempted when they are dragged away by their own evil desire and enticed. Then, after desire has conceived, it gives birth to sin; and sin, when it is full-grown, gives birth to death. Don't be deceived, my dear brothers and sisters. Every good and perfect gift is from above, coming

> down from the Father of the heavenly lights, who does not change like shifting shadows. He chose to give us birth through the word of truth that we might be a kind of first fruits of all he created.

Pray to resist temptations and to be delivered from evil. Pray every day for action, changes, and surviving the trials. James 1:2–4 says, "Consider it pure joy, my brothers and sisters, whenever you face trials of many kinds, because you know that the testing of your faith produces perseverance. Let perseverance finish its work so that you may be mature and complete, not lacking anything."

When we slide back or are cut down or persecuted, we can grow back stronger and braver. As with many plants (yuccas, thistles, petunias), when the top is cut off, the roots grow stronger and the top part grows thicker and more beautiful. This realization may take years. We can be encouraged as we consider what James 1:12 says, "Blessed is the one who perseveres under trial because, having stood the test, that person will receive the crown of life that the Lord has promised to those who love him."

We cannot change what happened, but we can change how we feel about it. We can change our habits of thinking. For example, if you have the habit of thinking "I can't," change to saying in your mind "I think I can. I think I can." Repeat this continuously as you try something like changing jobs, moving furniture or transferring to a new home: "I can do all this through Him who gives me strength" (Philippians 4:13).

It has been said, "When we are young, we want to change the world for God. When old, we want God to change the world for us." A friend said, "Hopefully by the time we are older we have learned that we can change ourselves and by doing that, the world around us may change. It is not our responsibility to change others. We leave that to God." Cancer taught her that "we cannot control what happens to us but we can control how we respond. God holds us responsible for the witness we present in all circumstances. He can do amazing things with our faithfulness, most of which we will never know." We can fight the tendency to be stuck on self. Rather than wanting to change God, we can be renewed by changing self.

We have a choice of looking to our painful past,

regretting mistakes, being overwhelmed with anxiety—or being renewed, made new every day, transformed. We can seek to grow younger while older. We may be depressed, as was Job, who said in Job 7:16, "I despise my life; I would not live forever. Let me alone; my days have no meaning." Or we can be renewed, healed, and spring forth.

We are told to accept God's love and presence, being content in want or plenty, and being thankful no matter the circumstances. A good reference is Philippians 4:12–13: "I know what it is to be in need, and I know what it is to have plenty. I have learned the secret of being content in any and every situation, whether well fed or hungry, whether living in plenty or in want. I can do all this through him who gives me strength."

Bitterness and complaints can be read in the book of Psalms. Yet the writers looked to God for change and help of various kinds. They acknowledged that their sins, bad habits, or distress were due to their own fault, for which they asked forgiveness.

We may have to change whom we are trying to please. In our work we may decide to achieve to our satisfaction in pleasing God, not our boss or audience.

So we pray:[16] "Change my heart, oh God. Make it ever true; Change my heart, oh God, may I be like you." Rejoice! God is with us as we change, giving us His transforming power.

Through the power of prayer, miracles happen. By praying for others, their attitudes, health, and openness to new possibilities can occur. They can feel the love sent by prayer. They can receive wisdom, courage, and strength through our prayerful requests. They can receive delights and gifts sent prayer-mail by us.

---

[16] Eddie Espinosa, "Change My Heart Oh God," based on Psalm 51:10. Copyright © 1982 Mercy Pub. Mercy/Vineyard.

Step 9:
For Opening Possibilities, Be Better, Not Bitter

Bitter or better—one letter difference with a change in attitude, a change in action, and with reading a verse or more every day, letting the Word penetrate our hearts. Bitterness is a barrier to being renewed daily. Bitterness is not the problem, but rather, staying bitter.

We can try to move from *getting mad* to *getting sad* at what a person has said or done. We can get angry and explode, attack the person verbally or physically, hurt ourselves, and seek revenge—or we can be calm and sad at what the person has done or left undone. We can pray to get through these trials.

We can put the crisis on the shelf temporarily a few minutes for the day and then increase time on the shelf each day after that. Put the pain or crisis on the shelf for one minute one day, then two minutes for two days, then three minutes for three days, and so on. Try to focus on Christ, not the crisis. We can center our lives on Christ rather than persons or offenses.

A crisis can be an opportunity to learn, change, or witness. The Chinese word for crisis are two symbols: opportunity and disaster.

Bitterness maintains hardness, and it distances one from God. It entertains the lies of Satan. We cannot glorify God in bitterness. It blinds one to opportunities. It causes one to make mistakes. It keeps one from doing things or talking with someone. Something may make us bitter because it accumulates with experiences of previous events or personal encounters. It adds to occurrences of the past, which makes us even more bitter. Bitterness blocks us from renewal and causes us to make bad decisions.

Wisdom and instructions are found in 1 Samuel 30:6: "David was in great danger; for the people spoke of stoning him, because all the people were bitter in spirit for their sons and daughters. But David strengthened himself in the Lord his God." (*NRSV* is used throughout Step 9.)

Other relevant Scriptures include the following:

- Job 10:1: "I loathe my life; I will give free utterance to my complaint. I will speak in the bitterness of my soul." (Verbalizing does help in healing.)

- Proverbs 14:10: "The heart knows its own bitterness, and no stranger shares its joy."

- Ephesians 4:31: "Put away from you all bitterness and wrath and anger and wrangling and slander, together with all malice."

- James 3:13–15: "Who is wise and understanding among you? Show by your good life that your works are done with gentleness born of wisdom. But if you have bitterness, envy, and selfish ambition in your hearts, do not be boastful and false to the truth. Such wisdom does not come down from above, but is earthly, unspiritual, and devilish."

A summary Scripture passage is Hebrews 12:14–15: "Make every effort to live in peace with everyone and to be holy; without holiness no one will see the Lord. See to it that no one falls short of the grace of

God and that no bitter root grows up to cause trouble and defiles many."

When we have allowed bitterness and mistakes to control our thoughts and self-image, we can seek renewal and healing through a prayer. Consider, for example, my prayer poem "Take the Bitter Memories."

> O God, I cannot sleep.
> I have no peace … bewailing mistakes, hurts, what could have been.
> O Lord, take the bitter memories from me, Lord;
> O Lord, let them be wisdom and strength through Thee, Lord;
> O Lord, turn them into joy for serving Thee, Lord;
> O Lord, take the bitter memories from me, Lord;
> Take my bad painful mistakes;
> So I am forgiven when I wake.
> Take my bitterness from the roots (Hebrews 12:14–15);
> Take my bitterness that defiles;
> Take my sins in thought, word, and deed.
> Take what I did and what I did not do.
> Take those unkind words
> Told to me and those I said.
> Take those bitter rejections.
> Take those angry curses.

Take those bad reputations,
Take my disappointments.
Take my failures and pains.
Forgive my crimes committed.
Forgive me for these, I pray.
Take the bitter memories from me
So I can sleep and live serenely
To arise each day more joyously! Amen.
And by the way, Lord,
Guide me to avoid making more mistakes. Amen.

Abandon bitterness and blame. Embrace new perspectives and increase self-esteem. Do not miss blessings because of your bitterness, long-held grudges, and curses. Pray every morning to receive a blessing to be a blessing to others. Give encouragement, a compliment, a statement of hope, a pat on the back, a smile, or a greeting.

Move from abandonment of bitterness to abundant living and sing "When Peace Like a River" by Horatio G. Spafford, *Gospel Hymns*. No. 2, 1876.

> When peace like a river, attendeth my way,
> When sorrows like sea billows roll.
> Whatever my lot, thou hast taught me to say,
> It is well, it is well with my soul.

Step 10:
Praise to Open a Window for God's Healing

We can open the window in the morning, open our heart, praise God, and join the birds in singing or humming. Psalm 98:1 says, "O Sing to the Lord a new song, for the marvelous things He has done." And consider Psalm 34:1–2: "I will extol the LORD at all times; his praise will always be on my lips. I will glory in the LORD; let the afflicted hear and rejoice." (This is not always easy for those in clinical depression.) We can sing[17] "This Is the Day the Lord Hath Made": "This is the day the Lord Hath Made. We will be glad and rejoice in it."

When in trouble, we can praise God. This opens up our hearts to receive God's gifts. I was in a tragic accident in Mexico while in a tour van, when a tire

---

[17] Dianne H. Gingrich, "This Is the Day the Lord Hath Made," based on Psalm 118:24. Copyright © 1975 by Dianne H. Risk.

blew. I saw my bloody arm. I recalled that I had heard in two separate churches to praise God when in trouble. I said, "There goes my piano career, but my *singing* career has just begun." So I started singing inwardly "Praise to the Lord, the Almighty."[18]

> Praise to the Lord, the Almighty, the King of creation! O my soul, praise him, for He is thy health and salvation! All ye who hear, now to God's temple draw near. Join me in glad adoration.

> Praise to the Lord, who o'er all things so wondrously reigneth, shelters thee under his wings, yea, so gently sustaineth. Hast thou not seen how the heart's wishes have been granted in what he ordained?

> Praise to the Lord, who doth prosper thy work and defend thee. Surely his

---

[18] Joachim Neander (lyricist), "Praise to the Lord, the Almighty" (1680), in *Chorale Book for England* (1863). Neander set the lyrics to music of Emeuerten Gesangbuch (1665).

goodness and mercy shall daily attend thee. Ponder anew what the Almighty can do, as with his love he befriends thee.

Praise to the Lord, oh, let all that is in me adore him! All that hath life and breath, come now with praises before him! Let the "amen" sound from God's people again; gladly forever adore him.

I had no pain, no fear. I was resting in the Lord.

Since my right hand had flown out the van's window from impact of a boulder to the window, it was too risky to try to attach it. My arm was amputated further when infected. Within one week of the accident, my son accessed the Internet and ordered piano music for the left hand only. Now I play almost any music on piano, keyboard, or organ, performing publicly. My hope was restored. Encouragement came when another son complimented me by saying, "You are doing better than last week." My hope was confirmed with Psalm 42:11: "Why are you cast down, O my soul, and why are you disquieted within me? Hope in God; for I shall again praise him, my help and my God." *(NRSV)*

Praise brings hope and assurance as in the song "Praise Him, Praise Him" by Fanny J. Crosby[19]:

> Praise him, praise him! Jesus, our blessed redeemer! Sing, O earth, his wonderful love proclaim! Hail him, hail him! Highest arch-angels in glory! Strength and honor give to his holy name!

> Like a shepherd, Jesus will guard his children. In his arms he carries them all day long. Praise him! praise him! Tell of his excellent greatness. [Refrain] Praise him! Praise him! ever in joyful song.

Praise and rejoice. God is with us no matter what. Pray for love and courage.

---

[19] Fanny J. Crosby (lyricist) and Chester G. Allen (composer), "Praise Him, Praise Him," in *Bright Jewels* (1869).

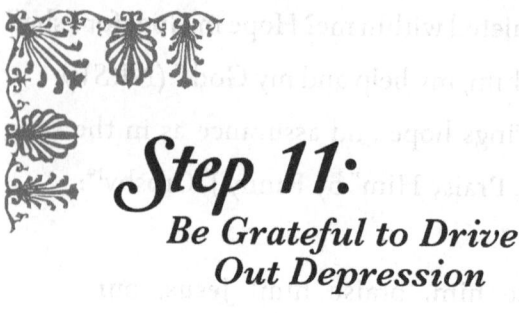

Step 11:
Be Grateful to Drive Out Depression

By giving thanks every day for everything to God, we are showing our commitment and central focus on God for receiving His gifts. Gratefulness renews us. I once heard that the place in the brain that involves depression cannot handle both depression and gratitude.

We can count on our fingers the gifts for which we are grateful, thankful, or blessed. Begin by naming one thing to be thankful for. Then name two in a row, three in a row, and so on. This helps us go to sleep.

Instructions are in the Bible: "Be joyful always; pray continually; give thanks in all circumstances, for this is God's will for you in Christ Jesus" (1 Thessalonians 5:16–18). *Giving thanks for everything* is hard to swallow unless we know the refining work is making us stronger and building character.

We remember the promise in Philippians 4:6–7 (*NKJV*): "Be anxious for nothing, but in everything by prayer and supplication, with thanksgiving, let your *requests* be made known to God; and the peace of God, which surpasses all understanding, will *guard* your hearts and minds through Christ Jesus" (emphasis mine).

Martin Rinkart's song "Now, Thank We All Our God" was written in the year when he conducted four thousand funerals, including his wife's, during the bubonic plague.[20] In another song, "Thanks to God for My Redeemer,"[21] August Ludwig Storm thanks God for the roses and for the thorns, for joy and for sorrow, for storms that he had weathered, for pain and for pleasure, for tears by now forgotten, for pleasant balmy springtime, for dark and dreary fall, for prayers answered and those denied, and for hope and peace. He wrote this song when he was on his back with great pain.

Persons feel affirmed and renewed when they hear

---

[20] As described in Robert J. Morgan, *Then Sings My Soul* (Thomas Nelson, 2003).

[21] August Ludwig Storm (lyricist), "Thanks to God for My Redeemer," trans. Carl E. Backstrom (1891). Public domain.

their name mentioned out loud, especially in prayer. It is also heartening to know others are supporting us in prayer, wherever they are. In 1 Timothy 1:12 *(NRSV)*, an example is: "I am grateful to Christ Jesus our Lord, who has strengthened me, because he judged me faithful and appointed me to his service." Also, 2 Timothy 1:3 says, "I am grateful to God—whom I worship with a clear conscience, as my ancestors did—when I remember you constantly in my prayers night and day."

Gratitude is mentioned in Acts 24:3 *(NRSV)*: "We welcome this in every way and everywhere with utmost gratitude." Again, in Colossians 3:16, we read: "Let the word of Christ dwell in you richly; teach and admonish one another in all wisdom; and with gratitude in your hearts sing psalms, hymns, and spiritual songs to God."

Let us continually thank God for His mercy, grace, goodness, kindness, faithfulness, wisdom, and presence. These are available to us and are new every morning. In suffering and persecution we rejoice because God is with us. We can pray that others, too, will receive these gifts.

Step 12:
Handle Worries and Be Yoked to the Lord, Who Carries Your Burdens

We have worries. Worrying is evidence we care. That is good. Too much worry is a barrier to renewal, to receiving the gifts for renewal, to healing, and to springing forth. We need to do something about our worry. We need to repent (turn, change) from worrying. That will break its power. "Work, don't worry" means doing something in spite of our worry.

Even the Scripture mentions that worrying cannot add years. In Matthew 6:25–29, Jesus says,

> Therefore I tell you, do not worry about your life, what you will eat or drink; or about your body, what you will wear. Is not life more than food, and the body more than clothes? Look at the birds of

the air; they do not sow or reap or store away in barns, and yet your heavenly Father feeds them. Are you not much more valuable than they? Can any one of you by worrying add a single hour to your life?

And why do you worry about clothes? See how the flowers of the field grow. They do not labor or spin. Yet I tell you that not even Solomon in all his splendor was dressed like one of these. If that is how God clothes the grass of the field, which is here today and tomorrow is thrown into the fire, will he not much more clothe you—you of little faith?

The greatest sin that many have is not trusting in God's power and goodness. We need to rest in the Lord. This is possible if we believe, as Jesus says in Matthew 11:28–30: "Come to me, all you who are weary and burdened, and I will give you rest. Take my yoke upon you and learn from me, for I am gentle and humble in heart, and you will find rest for your souls. For my yoke is easy and my burden is light." Responsibilities and burdens are lighter when shared. Yoked together, Jesus walks and works with you.

When we are responsible for something and it goes wrong, rather than going "to pieces" or in circles, we can be renewed by focusing on *the next steps to take*, as we seek God's wisdom. Identify the alternatives we have if something does not work out as we want. This will reduce worry's hold on us. Do not spend energy on wringing your hands in distress and bewilderment about what will happen. Rather, reach out and take the hand of God and list actions and resources for solving the problem.

Trusting and hoping in the Lord lead to renewal, healing, and springing forth. Psalm 40:1–4 *(CEB)* says it well:

> I put all my hope in the Lord. He leaned down to me; he listened to my cry for help. He lifted me out of the pit of death, out of the mud and filth, and set my feet on solid rock. He steadied my legs. He put a new song in my mouth, a song of praise for our God. Many will

> learn of this and be amazed; they will
> trust the Lord. Those who put their
> trust in the Lord, who pay no attention
> to the proud or to those who follow lies,
> are truly happy!

Trust is proclaimed in the song "You Are My Hiding Place."[22]

> You are my hiding place, You always
> fill my heart with songs of deliverance,
> Whenever I am afraid I will trust in You,
> I will trust in You, Let the weak say, "I
> am strong in the strength of the Lord."

Conditions for handling worries are in the song "Trust and Obey."[23]

> When we walk with the Lord in the
> light of his word, what a glory he sheds

---

[22] Michael Ledner, "You Are My Hiding Place," based on Psalm 31:19–20. Capitolcmglicensing.com. All rights reserved.

[23] John H. Sammis (lyricist) and Daniel B. Towner (composer), "Trust and Obey," in *Hymns Old and New* (1887).

on our way! While we do his good will, he abides with us still, and with all who trust and obey.

(Refrain) Trust and obey, for there's no other way to be happy in Jesus, but to trust and obey.

Not a burden we bear, not a sorrow we share, but our toil he doth richly repay. Not a grief nor a loss, not a frown nor a cross, but is bless'd if we trust and obey. (Go to refrain)

But we never can prove the delights of his love, until all on the altar we lay, for his favor he shows, and the joy he bestows, are for them who will trust and obey. (Go to refrain)

Then in fellowship sweet we will sit at his feet, or we'll walk by his side in the way. What he says we will do, where he sends we will go, never fear, only trust and obey. (Go to refrain)

Also, we read this exhortation in 1 Peter 5:7: "Cast all your anxiety on him because he cares for you." A promise is in the song "Cast Thy Burden upon the Lord."[24]

> Cast thy burden upon the Lord, and he shall sustain thee. He never will suffer the righteous to fall. He is at thy right hand. Thy mercy, Lord, is great, and far above the heav'ns. Let none be ashamed, that wait upon thee.

When we remove the material trash daily or weekly from our lives, we can sing "Cares Chorus."[25]

---

[24] Julius Schubring (lyricist), "*Eirf dein Anliegen auf den Herr* (Cast Thy Burden upon the Lord)," trans. William Bartholomew in *Elijah* (1846); music in *Neu-vermehrtes Gesangbuch* (1693), adapted by Felix Mendelssohn.

[25] Kelly Willard, "Cares Chorus," based on 1 Peter 5:7. Copyright © 1978 Maranatha! Music.

I cast all my cares upon You. I lay all of my burdens down at your feet; And anytime that I don't know what to do, I will cast all my cares upon You.

We rejoice, remembering God is with us. "Praise to the Lord, to God our Savior, who daily bears our burdens" (Psalm 68:19).

Step 13:
Handle Fear and Improve Faith

Fears are barriers to renewal unless we do something about them. It is normal to be fearful at times. It makes us cautious and preventive. We have fears from today and yesterday of all kinds. There are changes in our own lives and in the society that we do not understand. We have fears, felt every day, as our bodies change over time. We should remind ourselves daily, as written in the Scripture fifty-four times, not to be afraid. "Do not be afraid for I am with you. Do not be dismayed, for I am your God. I will strengthen you. I will help you. I will uphold you with my victorious right hand" (Isaiah 41:10 *NRSV*).

Fear can become sin if we do not take our fears to the Lord and do not live in trust. Jesus was fearful and sweated drops of blood. But He talked with God about His fears. (See Luke 22:24.) Read Deuteronomy 31:8.

We first must face our fears. Then try to reduce them. Some common fears are the unknowns, rumors, death, falling, rejection, failure, success, old age, violence, safety, getting ill, and financial security. Try to separate those that are real from those ungrounded. Jesus said in Luke 12:4-5, "I tell you, my friends, do not be afraid of those who kill the body and after that can do no more. But I will show you whom you should fear: Fear him who, after the killing of the body, has power to throw you into hell."

Make decisions based on faith, not fear. The outcome will be different. Psalm 34:4–6 says, "I sought the Lord, and he answered me; he delivered me from all my fears. Those who look to him are radiant; their faces are never covered with shame. This poor man called, and the Lord heard him; he saved him out of all his troubles." Read Jeremiah 51:46.

In Psalm 34:7–11 we read: "The angel of the Lord encamps around those who fear him, and he delivers them. Taste and see that the Lord is good; blessed is the one who takes refuge in him. Fear the Lord, you his holy people, for those who fear him lack nothing. The lions may grow weak and hungry, but those who seek the LORD LACK no good thing. Come, my children, listen to me; I will teach you the fear of the LORD."

A commitment is expressed well in "I Will Not Be Afraid."[26]

> I will not be afraid, I will not be afraid, I will look upward and travel onward. I will not be afraid.
>
> My Savior will be with me, My Savior will be with me, He goes before me and is beside me; So I am not afraid.
>
> His arms are underneath me, His arms are underneath me, His hand upholds me, His love enfolds me; So I am not afraid.
>
> His Word will stand forever. His truth shall guide me; it shall protect me; So I am not afraid.

---

[26] G. E. Govan and William Beery, "I Will Not Be Afraid" (1852), in *The Brethren Hymnal*. Music copyright © 1951, House of the Church of the Brethren, Elgin, IL.

Our call to 911 is Psalm 91:1-6, 9-12, 14-16. "He who dwells in the shelter of the Most High will rest in the shadow of the Almighty. I will say of the Lord, 'He is my refuge and my fortress, my God in whom I trust.' Surely he will save you from the fowler's snare and the deadly pestilence. He will cover you with his feathers, and under his wings you will find refuge; his faithfulness will be your shield and rampart. You will not fear the terror of night, nor the arrow that flies by night. If you make the Most High your dwelling-then no harm will befall you, no disaster will come near your tent. For he will command his angels to guard you in all your ways; they will lift you up in their hands, so that you will not strike your foot against a stone. 'Because he loves me,' says the Lord, 'I will rescue him; I will protect him, for he acknowledges my name. He will call upon me, and I will answer him; I will be with him in trouble. I will deliver him and honor him.'"

Step 14:
Be Productive—Keep Going But Also Keep Serving

Many times we pray to just keep going. But beyond that, we can pray to keep serving the Lord and our community. Serving is productive activity that renews us. Serving includes helping others to be renewed. This activity ranges from praying for someone while flat on one's back to preaching and baptizing those around the world. We can be productive in smiling, in praying, and in thanking others. Regardless of how young or old we are, we can be persons whom the lonely are seeking, persons who listen and understand.

> Even in old age they will produce fruit; they will remain vital and green, proclaiming, 'The Lord is upright; he is

my Rock, and there is no wickedness in him.' (Psalm 92:14–15 *NLT*)

We need a spiritual leader, pastor, inspiring friend, or someone who has faith in us. If only one person has faith in us, we can be productive.

A compliment keeps a person going for weeks. If no one else compliments you, compliment yourself for one thing you did well or for a good thought you had. Be encouraging as you talk with yourself. Remind yourself that you lived through other valleys and difficulties—so you will live through the current one. Repeat over and over, "God has helped me before, so I know He will help me through this time." Pray, "O Creator God, help me as You have helped before." After the task is completed, we can pray "Thank you, Jesus."

An old adage prevents us from making excuses of inadequacy. "God does not call the qualified but qualifies the called." And the Bible says that God will give us the words to say. Like the disciples, we ordinary people, filled with the Spirit, can do extraordinary things.

Read Scripture, poems, and hymns to delight in God's revelation and to meditate. We are told in Psalm 1:2-3 that if we read instructions in the Scriptures, finding delight in them, we will be productive, we will not wither, and we will prosper.

Billy Graham wrote, "The Bible is dotted with other examples of individuals whom God used in their later years—men and women who refused to use old age as an excuse to ignore what God wanted them to do."[27]

The song "We Would Be Building"[28] is a commitment to productivity.

> We would be building; temples still undone O'er crumbling walls their crosses scarcely lift; Waiting till love can raise the broken stone, And hearts creative bridge the human rift; We would be building, Master, let Thy plan Reveal the life that God would give to man.

---

[27] *Nearing Home: Life, Faith, and Finishing Well* (Nashville, TN: Thomas Nelson), 13. Copyright © 2011.

[28] Purd E. Deitz (lyricist), "We Would Be Building." Words copyright © 1936; copyright © James Deitz, 109 Hickory Hollow Court, Amherst, OH 44001. All rights reserved; used with permission. Music by Jean Sibelius (tune of Finland). Copyright by Breitkopf & Hartel, Wiesbaden, Germany. Musical arrangement copyright © 1933 by the Presbyterian Board of Christian Education: renewed 1961.

O keep us building, Master; may our hands Nee'er falter when the dream is in our hearts, When to our ears there come divine commands And all the pride of sinful will departs; We build with Thee, O grant enduring worth Until the heavenly kingdom comes on earth.

A verse that proclaims our source of power—God—uses the vine to explain our need to be connected:

> "I am the true vine, and my Father is the gardener. He cuts off every branch in me that bears no fruit, while every branch that does bear fruit he prunes so that it will be even more fruitful. You are already clean because of the word I have spoken to you. Remain in me, and I will remain in you. No branch can bear fruit by itself, it must remain in the vine. Neither can you bear fruit unless you remain in me. I am the vine; you are the branches. If a man remains

in me and I in him, he will bear much fruit; apart from me you can do nothing. If anyone does not remain in me, he is like a branch that is thrown away and withers…If you remain in me and my words in you, ask whatever you wish, and it will be given you." (John 15:1-7)

A productive life is a fruitful life by planting the seed, although God and others who provide nourishment may see the yield. A productive life points out possible paths, prepares a path, or shows new purposes. It shows alternatives, tells consequences, gives resources, or shows resources for development.

Your reward is being told, "Well done, good and faithful servant! "Well done, good and faithful servant! You have been faithful with a few things; I will put you in charge of many things. Come and share your master's happiness" (Matthew 25:21).

Step 15:
Associate with Godly, Positive People for Progress

Associate with positive people because associating only with negative people is a barrier to renewal. As indicated in Psalm 1:1–3 (NKJV), avoid those who would sneer at you, mock you, or drag you down: "Blessed is the man who walks not in the counsel of the ungodly, nor stands in the path of sinners, nor sits in the seat of the scornful; But his delight is in the law of the Lord, And in His law he meditates day and night. He shall be like a tree planted by the rivers of water, That brings forth its fruit in its season, Whose leaf also shall not wither, And whatever he does shall prosper. You will be like a tree planted by living water."

And Hebrews 12:1 says, "Therefore, since we are surrounded by such a great cloud of witnesses, let us throw off everything that hinders and the sin that so easily entangles. And let us run with perseverance the race marked out for us."

We have a crowd of living witnesses as we struggle to renew life. Mine include my podiatrist, kidney specialist, ophthalmologist, gynecologist, oncologist, oxygen therapist, dentist, hair designer (Chris Love), supportive persons at church, kind relatives, familiar service workers, cleaning lady (Martha Castro), reviewers and editors, pastors, my children, my husband (my primary caregiver) and others who care or help me.

We need to constantly encourage each other at home, work, and church or in the community—every day, every time we meet. We can encourage simply by asking about their mission rather than just asking about one's health. We can simply smile at strangers, which encourages them and us. We can literally pat someone on the back and do other kind acts.

Positive people who pray for us as we go through a crisis give us strength. Many report they feel closer to God when others pray for them. Sharing troubles and fears with a trusted friend or professional helps in our renewal. When sharing or asking for prayers, we verbalize our inner doubts, fears, and regrets. (However, not every counselor or minister is the right one for a particular individual.)

A Chinese proverb says, "When we share our troubles, we halve them. When we share our joys, we double them." Chinese proverbs are verbally passed among generations.

In Philippians 4:8–9 *(NRSV)* we read, "Finally, beloved, whatever is true, whatever is honorable, whatever is just, whatever is pure, whatever is pleasing, whatever is commendable, if there is any excellence and if there is anything worthy of praise, think about these things. Keep on doing the things that you have learned and received and heard and seen in me, and the God of peace will be with you." A hymn called "Look for the Beautiful"[29] is based on those verses.

> Look for the beautiful, look for the true;
> Sunshine and shadow are all around you;
> Looking at evil, we grope in the night;
> Looking at Jesus, we walk in the light;
> Look for the beautiful, honor the right.

---

[29] F. E. Belden, "Look for the Beautiful" (1900), in *The Brethren Hymnal*. Copyright © 1951, House of the Church of the Brethren, Elgin, IL.

> Think of the beautiful, think of the true;
> Tho'ts like an avalanche sweep over you;
> Keep not the multitude, sort them with care;
> Testing by purity, purging by prayer;
> Think of the beautiful, think of the fair.

Focusing on the good and the beautiful may require switching TV channels or changing magazines. Join a carefully chosen support group from church or community. Read about godly people in the Bible. We can read inspiring biographies that inspire and challenge. These can help form our new identity. However, we still need to help and be a positive influence to those who are lost, knocked down, bitter, or discouraged.

A song based on Psalm 1 is "How Bless'd Are They."[30] (Remember, *blessed* means *happy*.)

> How bless'd are they who, fearing God,
> from sin restrain their feet, who will not
> with the wicked stand, who shun the
> scorner's seat.

---

[30] "How Bless'd Are They" (author unknown), published in *Psalter* (1912). Music: *The CL Psalms of David* (1615).

How bless'd are they who make God's law their treasure delight, and meditate upon that word with gladness day and night.

The way of sinners, far from God, shall surely be o'er-thrown. But God will guard the righteous well; their way is watched and known.

The issue is remaining Godly while associating with and reaching out to negative, marginalized, and sinful persons. We are to uplift the down-trodden, broken people.

Rejoice! We can overcome the evil, be empowered in helping ourselves and others in paths of abundant and beautiful living. Be strong in the Lord!

Step 16:
Handle Anger So It Will Not Choke You

At various times, we have more opportunity to reflect. Emotions which were latent for years begin to emerge, to haunt and cripple us. We have been busy with job, children, and other matters, but when older, we may have to deal with anger and other painful memories or words that were said.

The Bible tells us that Jesus had anger. God has anger. However, too much anger, if it controls us, is a barrier for renewal. James 1:20 says, "For your anger does not produce God's righteousness." (*NRSV* is used throughout Step 16.)

Anger is good when it motivates us to change a particular thing or change ourselves. Further, our anger can be funneled into creative works when we do something or build something. These include works such as a creating a scholarship memorial, taking up a cause, or implementing a new project. Big hurts often require working through anger to do something positive.

Anger is in the list of sins that prevent us from eternal life. Scripture warns us in the gospel of Matthew and the book of Galatians.

> For I tell you, unless your righteousness exceeds that of the scribes and Pharisees, you will never enter the kingdom of heaven. You have heard that it was said to those of ancient times, "You shall not murder"; and "whoever murders shall be liable to judgment." But I say to you that if you are angry with a brother or sister, you will be liable to judgment; and if you insult a brother or sister, you will be liable to the council; and if you say, "You fool," you will be liable to the hell of fire. (Matthew 5:21–22)

> Now the works of the flesh are obvious: fornication, impurity, licentiousness,

idolatry, sorcery, enmities, strife, jealousy, anger, quarrels, dissensions, factions, envy, drunkenness, carousing, and things like these. I am warning you, as I warned you before: those who do such things will not inherit the kingdom of God. (Galatians 5:19–21)

A command in Scripture is to rid oneself of anger, as said in Colossians 3:8: "But now you must get rid of all such things—anger, wrath, malice, slander, and abusive language from your mouth."

Unresolved anger near the time of offense may result in accumulation with other events and explodes inappropriately and dangerously.

Additional wisdom and instructions about controlling anger are found in the Bible:

- James 1:19: "You must understand this, my beloved: let everyone be quick to listen, slow to speak, slow to anger."

- Ephesians 4:26: "Be angry but do not sin; do not let the sun go down on your anger."

- Ephesians 4:31: "Put away from you all bitterness and wrath and anger and wrangling and slander, together with all malice."

In Proverbs 12:16, we are told: "Fools show their anger at once, but the prudent ignore an insult." And Proverbs 14:29 says, "Whoever is slow to anger has great understanding, but one who has a hasty temper exalts folly." Other verses about governing anger wisely include the following:

- Proverbs 15:1: "A soft answer turns away wrath, but a harsh word stirs up anger."

- Proverbs 15:18: "Those who are hot-tempered stir up strife, but those who are slow to anger calm contention."

- Proverbs 16:32: "One who is slow to anger is better than the mighty, and one whose temper is controlled than one who captures a city."

- Proverbs 19:11: "Those with good sense are slow to anger, and it is their glory to overlook an offense."

- Proverbs 29:11: "A fool gives full vent to anger, but the wise quietly holds it back."

Good advice about anger helps keep peace among friends and strangers. We can choose to not fight every battle. Ecclesiastes 7:21–22 says, "Do not pay attention to every word people say, or you may hear your servant cursing you—for you know in your heart that many times you yourself have cursed others." Proverbs 22:24 says, "Make no friends with those given to anger, and do not associate with hotheads."

And Proverbs 29:22 states, "One given to anger stirs up strife, and the hot head causes much transgression."

Strife occurs when one harbors insults, twists the words people say, or takes the words the wrong way.

The process for handling anger suggested by pastor Charles Stanley[31] is as follows:

1. Identify the source, such as: past hurt; rejection; didn't deal with it; resentment.

2. Be willing to confess the anger.

---

[31] Based on my notes from the Charles Stanley television program *In Touch*, aired May 25, 2013.

3. Clarify feelings, such as: hurt; rejected; needs not met. Deal with it quickly, because the longer you don't the longer you preserve and justify it.

4. Take an emotional time-out. Stop and think—true or not? Why?

5. Don't respond to all acts and everything someone says about you, even if hurtful or unjust things.

6. Put anger away. Forgive people. Lay it down again and again. If you don't, you play into the hands of others.

7. Ask God to replace anger, to get you out of that mood.

8. Benefit from it. Do something worthwhile. Don't live with poisons—all kinds.

9. Set your heart with purpose. Prevent anger from reoccurring. Not dealing with it can threaten your present life and eternal life. It is self-destructive and disastrous. That is not worth it.

10. Become a strong witness to the power and peace of God.

A prayer hymn entitled "Lord, Speak to Me" helps us deal with anger.[32] "Lord, speak to me, that I may speak in living echoes of Thy tone; As Thou hast sought, so let me seek Thine erring children lost and lone." Another prayer hymn for handling anger is "Dear Lord and Father of Mankind."[33] "Breathe through the heats of our desire Thy coolness and Thy balm; Let sense be dumb, let flesh retire; Speak through the earthquake, wind, and fire, O still small voice of calm!"

I wrote a poem called "Be Still and Know That I AM God," which expresses the calm. It is founded on Psalm 46:10, Psalm 37:7, and Mark 4:39.

> *Be still, I was told,*
> *But I resented it.*
> *Couldn't sit still,*

---

[32] Frances R. Havergal (1836–1879) and Robert Schumann (1810–1856), "Lord, Speak to Me," in *The Brethren Hymnal*. Copyright © 1951, House of the Church of the Brethren, Elgin, IL.

[33] John Greenleaf Whittier and Fredrick Maker, "Dear Lord and Father of Mankind," in *The Brethren Hymnal*. Copyright © 1951, House of the Church of the Brethren, Elgin, IL.

Yearning to squirm.
Couldn't be still,
Wanting to run.
Couldn't be still,
Aching to talk,
Balking, not talking,
Couldn't be still.
Had to fight, get revenge, get even.
Couldn't let God be in control.
Couldn't let Christ show me the way.
Couldn't be still and hear Christ.
Couldn't be still and feel Christ.
Couldn't let the Spirit pervade
With love and calmness!
The Spirit finally prayed
With sighs beyond words.
I surrendered in stillness.
Strength, wisdom, and hope
Invaded my soul!
Power and peace
Invaded my stillness.

Step 17:
Change Scenery—
Visible and Invisible

A change in scenery seems to revitalize, renew. A pediatrician even recommended taking a trip, which could aid a child's recovery from certain illnesses. Walk around the block, take a different route home from work, travel, or take a peaceful drive. This can reduce stress and may calm the soul.

We can rearrange the furniture so that we change our view and get a different perspective than before. If a spouse or loved one living with us has died, we might replace the chair that person used and change the layout of the other furniture, for example. Changing pictures on the wall or something in the front or back yards also helps.

By volunteering in organizations, we not only change scenery, but also we get a new purpose, identity, associations, and physical activity. There we do acts of kindness.

We can design and use a prayer garden or chair that changes our daily discipline. Jesus and His disciples went to a certain place to pray every day. My three-year-old grandson, after hearing a sermon of mine, said, "I feel God in my bed."

A friend sent me this suggestion: "When someone is confined to a room, bed, or other limited mobility (whether by lack of movement, sight, etc.), they can still visualize themselves in their favorite place and transport themselves there, perhaps for a chat with Jesus, and enjoy the time and place without ever leaving their spot. An imaginary trip to your 'happy place' can restore and refresh."

See the majesty, the balance, the beauty in God's handiwork by looking into the center of a flower. In the 1970s, when farmers were stressed from losing a farm, perhaps in the family for generations, educators at Purdue University wrote a series of leaflets to reduce stress. One such leaflet told them to stare into the center of a flower. This alters our focus, gives us a change in scenery, and renews by experiencing beauty.

Isaiah 51:3 is relevant: "The LORD will surely comfort Zion and will look with compassion on all her ruins; he will make her deserts like Eden, her wastelands like the garden of the LORD. Joy and gladness will be found in her, thanksgiving and the sound of singing." Another verse on beauty and joy is Isaiah 61:3: "And provide for those who grieve in Zion—to bestow on them a crown of beauty instead of ashes, the oil of joy instead of mourning, and a garment of praise instead of a spirit of despair. They will be called oaks of righteousness, a planting of the LORD for the display of his splendor."

In 2 Corinthians 5:17 (*NRSV*): we read: "So if anyone is in Christ, there is a new creation; everything old has passed away; see, everything has become new!" To help in becoming new, we can sing "God, Who Touches Earth."[34]

> God, who touches earth with beauty,
> make my heart anew. With your Spirit
> recreate me pure and strong and true.
>
> Like your springs and running waters,
> make me crystal pure. Like your rocks

---

[34] Mary S. Edgar, "God, Who Touches Earth" (1925). Copyright © 1939 Estate of Mary S. Edgar, c/o Gail McChesney, 606-1901 Pilgrims Way, Oakville, ON L6M 2W9. All rights reserved. Used with permission.

of towering grandeur, make me strong and sure.

Like your dancing waves in sunlight, make me glad and free. Like the straightness of the pine trees, let me upright be.

Like the arching of the heavens, lift my thoughts above. Turn my dreams to noble action, ministries of love.

God, who touches earth with beauty, make my heart anew. Keep me ever by your Spirit, pure and strong and true.

Step 18:
Do Acts of Kindness

God is kind. Therefore, if we are renewed to be more in the image of God, we are more kind. We can do intentional and random acts of kindnesses each day, such as thanking and smiling to a service worker. Kindnesses include any type of help or pleasant surprises. The Association of Christians in Social Work has this slogan: "Be a little kinder than you think necessary because everyone is fighting some kind of battle."[35]

An eighty-year-old woman learned to repair jewelry. She did this for people who gave her something in exchange. One friend gave her gifts of homemade pastries, an act of kindness. Now it has expanded into a business for the friend. This is an example of how learning something new can renew us. Another woman

---

[35] The slogan is attributed to both T. H. Thompson and John Watson.

washes people's eyeglasses with a wipe—whoever she meets, whenever. Another one helps people when they have car trouble. Letting someone get in line before you is an act of kindness. Others show kindness by listening to someone in distress, just being there beside the person to listen, or by making a phone call.

Other kindnesses shown are hospitality, a man taking off his coat and giving it to a cold man sitting near the sidewalk, giving unused clothes away, helping people to put on their coat or jacket, praying with a person instantly rather than saying "I will pray for you."

Concentrate on doing for others. There are a multitude of opportunities in the various charitable organizations that serve our communities. Volunteers with all levels of skill are desperately needed, from the ninety-year-old who holds babies in a day care center to the former CEO who serves on the board of a Christian drug rehab organization. If you cannot stand for hours preparing food in the soup kitchen, maybe you could sit and catalog medications in the free clinic. Another woman suggests, "Don't expect opportunities to do something you enjoy to come knocking. Go out and look for them." Be open to the Spirit using everyday simple opportunities to do random acts of kindness. "Ask," "seek," and "knock" (Matthew 7:7; Luke 11:9).

Other examples of acts of kindness include the following: calling on the phone; lending presence at the bedside; doing something for survivors; paying a higher tip; paying the bridge toll for the car behind you; praying for those on the prayer line; relieving caregivers; blessing people spiritually, silently, or audibly; giving your coat to a stranger; providing a box of goodies for someone in the hospital every day; and spontaneous acts. An appropriate hymn is "Help Us to Help Each Other."[36]

> Help us to help each other, Lord, each other's load to bear, that all may live in true accord, our joys and pains to share.
>
> Help us to build each other up, your strength within us prove. Increase our faith, confirm our hope, and fill us with your love …

---

[36] Charles Wesley, "Help Us to Help Each Other," in *Hymns and Sacred Poems* (1742). Revised in *Hymns for Today's Church* (1982). Copyright © 1982, Hope Publishing Co.

... Drawn by the magnet of your love we find our hearts made new. Nearer each other let us move, and nearer still to you.

A commitment song is "I Would Be True"[37]: I would be true, for there are those who trust me; I would be pure, for there are those who care; I would be strong, for there is much to suffer; I would be brave, for there is much to dare.

I would be friend of all, the foe, the friendless; I would be giving and forget the gift; I would be humble, for I know my weakness. I would look up, and laugh, and love, and lift.

---

[37] Howard A. Walter and Joseph Barnby, "I Would Be True" (in public domain), published in *Brethren Hymnal*, copyright © 1951, House of the Church of the Brethren, Elgin, IL.

Step 19:
Lift Loneliness to the Light

Loneliness afflicts many people in many different situations. Some are lonely while in a crowd. It may be greater in old age for those not being renewed daily. Mother Teresa of Calcutta, the famous Catholic sister who ministered to the poor of India, said, "Loneliness and the feeling of being uncared for and unwanted are the greatest poverty." Pentz said, "Loneliness is being unaware of the One who is with us everywhere."[38] And, "Many Christians suffer from loneliness because they are sitting instead of serving." So we endeavor to take action: pursuing interests that develop mind, body, and soul; trying one new thing or place each week; pursuing peace; and building courage and bravery.

---

[38] Croft M. Pentz, *The Complete Book of Zingers*. Copyright © 1990, Tyndale House.

A prayer is Psalm 25:16: "Turn to me and be gracious to me, for I am lonely and afflicted." We can be productive to solve loneliness. Other activities to overcome loneliness include the following:

- Use time for healthy reflection and creative endeavors;
- Enjoy being alone with God;
- Write your new overall purpose for living from day to day;
- Identify your needs and longings;
- Fight the temptation toward unhealthy habits or idle pursuits;
- Exercise or walk;
- Plan a day or evening out;
- Smile and be friendly;
- Volunteer;
- Help someone less fortunate;
- Take study courses;
- Find another lonely person with whom you can talk on the phone every day (this is a good security check, also); and
- Join one of the many kinds of support groups.

We can work at keeping loneliness and feelings of being unwanted to a minimum. Reminders of friends and what they said, did, or made through the years can be seen each day in your home. Include today's gift from them when "counting your blessings" at night when loneliness is strongest.

To combat the feelings of neglect or being unwanted and uncared for, the song "What a Friend We Have in Jesus"[39] helps us. It expresses the need to have a spiritual conversation as well as finding someone with whom to talk about needs and concerns.

> What a friend we have in Jesus, all our sins and griefs to bear! What a privilege to carry everything to God in prayer! Oh, what peace we often forfeit, oh, what needless pain we bear, all because we do not carry everything to God in prayer.

---

[39] Joseph M. Scriven, "What a Friend We Have in Jesus" (1855), in *Spirit Minstrel: A Collection of Hymns and Music* (1857). Alt. music: Williams P. Rolands (1916) or Charles C. Converse (1868) in *Silver Wings* (1870).

Have we trials and temptations? Is there trouble anywhere? We should never be discouraged—take it to the Lord in prayer! Can we find a friend so faithful, who will all our sorrows share? Jesus knows our every weakness—take it to the Lord in prayer!

Are we weak and heavy laden, 'cumbered with a load of care? Precious Savior, still our refuge, take it to the Lord in prayer! Do thy friends despise, forsake thee? Take it to the Lord in prayer! In his arms he'll take and shield thee—thou will find a solace there.

Enlightenment for dealing with loneliness is in the Scriptures. In Hebrews 13:5–6 it says, "Keep your lives free from the love of money and be content with what you have, because God has said, 'Never will I leave you, never will I forsake you.' So we say with confidence. 'The Lord is my helper; I will not be afraid. What can mere mortals do to me?'"

The benefits of turning to God to help with loneliness are mentioned in Scripture. Psalm 25:16 says, "Turn to me and be gracious to me, for I am lonely and afflicted." And 1 Timothy 5:5 says, "The widow who is really in need and left all alone puts her hope in God and continues night and day to pray and to ask God for help."

God turns to us to alleviate the burdens of our loneliness. Numbers 11:17 says, "I will come down and speak with you there, and I will take some of the power of the Spirit that is on you and put it on them. They will share the burden of the people with you so that you will not have to carry it alone." And in John 15:18–19, Jesus states, "If the world hates you, be aware that it hated me before it hated you. If you belonged to the world, the world would love you as its own. Because you do not belong to the world, but I have chosen you out of the world—therefore the world hates you."

We can change our attitude to help with loneliness. In Romans 14:6–8 we read: "Whoever regards one day as special does so to the Lord. Whoever eats meat does so to the Lord, for they give thanks to God; and whoever abstains does so to the Lord and gives thanks to

God. For none of us lives for ourselves alone, and none of us dies for ourselves alone. If we live, we live for the Lord; and if we die, we die for the Lord. So, whether we live or die, we belong to the Lord."

Some counselors suggest we should recognize our need for others and that others need us for their own renewal. These experts suggest we organize our lives so that we interact with people every day. It may be going to the grocery store to be a witness or give a smile. It may be interacting with a person who would be lonely without you, to chat at a specific time every day. Or praying with someone from a nearby apartment at a given time each day. This is a time to share wisdom, experiences, and love of Jesus and ourselves, for constant renewal.

Remember the opportunity in Revelation 3:20: "Here I am! I stand at the door and knock. If anyone hears my voice and opens the door, I will come and eat with him, and he with me."

Here is a prayer[40] we can say for those who are lonely: "Lord Jesus Christ, we praise You and love You!

---

[40] Fr. Joseph Mary Wolfe, MFVA, *EWTN Family Prayer* (Irondale, AL: EWTN Catholic Publishing), A22. © 2011 EWTN Catholic Publishing.

You call us friends, and Your friends we wish to be! Console those who are lonely by making known to them Your Presence. Let the love of Your Sacred Heart give them consolation. Bring into their lives good friends who will help them grow in loneliness. Show them how to be a good friend to those who are in need. Make them rich in charity, ready to serve others."

Amen.

Step 20:
Breathe for Healing of Body and Renewing of Spirit

"Breathe on Me, Breath of God" is a prayer hymn for healing, renewing, and springing forth.[41] "Breathe on me, Breath of God. Fill me with life anew. That I may love what thou doest love and do what thou wouldst do." Another hymn is "Breathe."[42] "This is the air I breathe, this is the air I breathe, Your Holy Presence living in me. This is my daily bread, this is my daily bread, Your very Word spoken to me."

A wonderful possibility for us is reported in John

---

[41] Edwin Hatch (lyricist), "Breathe on Me, Breath of God" (1878), music by Robert Jackson (1888), in *Hymnal: A Worship Book.* Copyright © 1992. Brethren Press, Elgin, IL.

[42] Marie Barnett, "Breathe" (1995). Copyright © 1995 EMI Music Publishing, Universal Publishing Group, and Kobat Music Publishing Ltd. Music Services. Mercy/Vineyard. All rights reserved. Used with permission.

20:22: "When he had said this, he breathed on them and said to them, 'Receive the Holy Spirit.'"

A breathing exercise not only heals and renews us, but also it can unite us with the Holy Spirit. If we cannot sleep, are scared, are stressed, or are in a new experience, we can practice controlled, deep breathing with selected words. For example, in our mind we can state and repeat the phrase "into the ... arms of Jesus," inhaling as we start and exhaling as we visualize being in the arms of Jesus. Relax and sink deeper each time into the arms of Jesus. When my granddaughter asked how I felt about dying, I said I did not fear because Jesus would lift me up in his arms. Now I sense His arms around me all day. Other examples of controlled breathing to invoke the Holy Spirit, bringing calmness and control, repeatedly breathing slowly in and slowly out, are as follows:

- Breathe in on "Power ..." and out on "Peace," then relax, and repeat.
- Breathe in on "Strength ..." and out on "Peace," then relax, and repeat.

- For a sense of renewal or cleansing, inhale while saying "In with Jesus …" and exhale on "Out with Satan."
- Similarly, "In with more oxygen … Out with more carbon dioxide." (Like mountain climbers do, breathe in with nose, out with mouth.)
- "In with love … out with hate and bitterness."
- "In with goodness … out with badness."

If ever you are severely anxious, scared, or nervous, breathe deeply three times, saying "In the name of the Father, Son, and Holy Spirit."

Beyond praying, breathe every moment for wisdom and redemption: "In with the Spirit…(hold) out with weakness…(hold)."

A second grade teacher with home and school responsibilities was full of anxiety and stress, even hyperventilating. When she breathed deeply and held it, she became calm and collected. Another person with at the end of the year with moving boxes all around became so stressed that her legs were moving out of control and out of sync with her breathing. The doctor was called. She vowed to never let that happen again.

She now breathes in the name of the Father, the Son, and Holy Spirit.

"A Prayer for Pentecost"[43] is appropriate:

> You who blow about us,
> Both gently, and in ways that annoy us,
> Continue to breathe new life into us.
> Continue to guide, or even push us.
> We can take getting our hair messed up,
> If we know it will be for a good cause.
> With each breath we take,
> Fill us ever so much more
> With your love and all things good,
> That we might be a part of helping another.
> Breathe more easily, more calmly,
> More in rhythm, with you.
> In the name of Jesus,
> Whose every breath offers hope and peace,
> Amen.

Rejoice! The Spirit is with us in every breath we take.

---

[43] Erin Matteson, "A Prayer for Pentecost," in a newsletter of Church of the Brethren (2013). Matteson is a pastor in Modesto, CA.

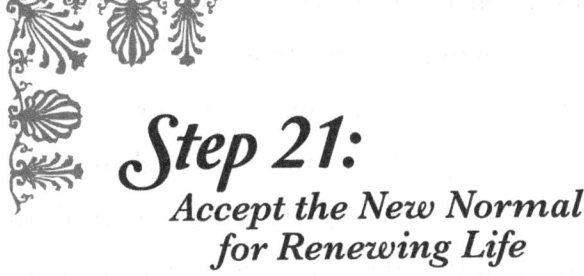

Step 21:
Accept the New Normal for Renewing Life

*A*ccept normal changes with different stages of life. Or accept unexpected developments that we cannot change. Someone who has a serious injury or illness at any age can benefit from this advice.

Recovery from a health setback (or gracefulness in growing older) is evidenced by standing in front of a mirror, naked, and being able to laugh. Laughing is medicine, as Proverbs 17:22 (*NLT*) attests: "A cheerful heart is good medicine, but a broken spirit saps a person's strength." Laughing can bring pink to pale cheeks and helps to hide any dark circles under eyes.

A friend told me she began to embrace her "new normal" and was grateful, once again, for another day of life. It is mind over matter and if you do not mind, it does not matter. Every day, we say we will be better next week, when in reality, as the Second Corinthians verse says, our bodies are "wasting away."

Accepting the "new normal" helps us as we go through the valleys of shadows and the shadows of death. Expect these and expect, as the Twenty-Third Psalm says, that the Good Shepherd will be with us. His goodness and mercy follow us, chase us, and want to be with us whom He created. The plaque on my desk before and after my severe accident says, "The Lord did not promise that life would be easy but did promise to be with us each step of the way." (Isaiah 43)

The *new normal* expression was used by Piper[44]:

> Human nature has a tendency to try to reconstruct old ways and pick up where we left off. If we're wise, we won't continue to go back to the way things were (we can't anyway). We must instead forget the old standard and accept a "new normal." … I had to adjust and accept my physical limitations as part of my new normal. … At some point in our lives,

---

[44] Don Piper and Cecil Murphey, *90 Minutes in Heaven*, 137–41. Copyright © 2004, Revell, Grand Rapids, MI.

> some of us want to go back to a simpler, healthier, or happier time. We can't but we still keep dreaming about how it once was. ... There are things I will never be able to do again. ... The sooner I make peace with that fact and accept the way things are, the sooner I'll be able to live in peace and enjoy my new normalcy.

Rather than dwelling on the things we cannot do, we can make a list of the things we can do. An example is that I can't plant flowers but I can still smell them. When Piper did this process, he found over one thousand things he still could do. He realized he had more going for him than he had thought. He said, "I had focused so heavily on my losses that I had forgotten what I had left. And I hadn't realized the opportunities I might never have tried otherwise."

When I had my critical accident, someone asked the minister in Mexico how I would survive. He said I would adjust to losing my hand because I focused on the internal and eternal more than the physical. Embrace the *new normal* that results from change. Our bodies change as we get older. We have fears—felt everyday as our body changes, we lose hearing or sight, and we have aches and pains. Accept these as normal and that we will have unknowns that cause fear. We will walk through the shadows of death continually. Rather than hoping to always be restored to former health, activities, happiness, let us hope we can accept the new normal and continue to serve in spite of new obstacles or our limitations.

Accepting the new normal, for some older people, involves being dependent on other people as well as on God. In John 21:17b-18 Jesus, after His resurrection, says to Peter: "Very truly I tell you, when you were younger you dressed yourself and went where you wanted; but when you are old you will stretch out your hands, and someone else will dress you and lead you where you do not want to go." A prayer is Psalm 71:9: "Do not cast me off in the time of old age; do not forsake me when my strength is spent."

Although we are dependent on others, we can still be in control of our feelings we hold inside. If frightened in dependency or other situations, remember that we have the Holy Spirit to be our advocate—spiritually, legally, or in both respects. Several verses support this promise. In Job 16:19 we read, "Even now my witness is in heaven; my advocate is on high." Other instructive verses include the following:

- John 14:16: "And I will ask the Father, and he will give you another advocate to help you and be with you forever."

- John 14:26: "But the Advocate, the Holy Spirit, whom the Father will send in my name, will teach you all things and will remind you of everything I have said to you."

- John 15:26: "When the Advocate comes, whom I will send to you from the Father—the Spirit of truth who goes out from the Father—he will testify about me."

- John 16:7: "But very truly I tell you, it is for your good that I am going away. Unless I go away, the Advocate will not come to you; but if I go, I will send him to you."

Of course, Jesus also advocates. As the first letter of John says, "My dear children, I write this to you so that you will not sin. But if anybody does sin, we have an Advocate with the Father—Jesus Christ, the Righteous One" (1 John 2:1).

Accepting the *new normal* is the key. Counting the things you can still do is a daily practice for renewal, healing, and springing forth. Peace comes with acceptance, which the song "O God in Restless Living"[45] conveys:

> O God in restless living we lose our spirits' peace. Calm our unwise confusion, bid Thou our clamor cease. Let anxious hearts grow quiet, like pools at evening still, till Thy reflected heavens all our spirits fill.
>
> Teach us, beyond our striving, the rich rewards of rest. Who does not live serenely is never deeply blest. O tranquil, radiant Sunlight, bring Thou our lives to flower, less wearied with our effort, more aware of power.

---

[45] Harry Emerson Fosdick (b. 1878), "O God in Restless Living." Words used by permission for *The Brethren Hymnal*, copyright © 1951, House of the Church of the Brethren, Elgin, IL.

Step 22:
Stand on the Promises for Strength

Remember the promises and Scripture verses that give us renewal, comfort, and strength. Repeat them often. Each day, choose a promise that guides and supports you. (*NRSV* is used throughout Step 22.)

We are reminded in 2 Corinthians 1:20 as follows: "For in him every one of God's promises is a 'Yes.' For this reason it is through him that we say the 'Amen,' to the glory of God." The next guidance is in 2 Corinthians 7:1: "Since we have these promises, beloved, let us cleanse ourselves from every defilement of body and spirit, making holiness perfect in the fear of God." The importance of Jesus' coming to earth is revealed in Hebrews 8:6: "But Jesus has now obtained a more excellent ministry, and to that degree he is the mediator of a better covenant, which has been enacted through better promises." And 2 Peter 1:4 provides the following application: "Thus he has given us, through these things, his precious and very great promises, so that through them you may escape from the corruption that is in the world because of lust, and may become participants of the divine nature."

Among the promises from which we can choose each day is "Your hope is in the Lord. Your joy is in the Lord." Another is "Be still and know that 'I Am' your God" (Psalm 46:10). " 'Do not be afraid of them, for I am with you and will rescue you,' declares the Lord" (Jeremiah 1:8).

We can sing the song "Standing on the Promises."[46]

> Standing on the promises that cannot fail when the howling storms of doubt and fear assail. By the living word of God I shall prevail—standing on the promises of God.
>
> Standing on the promises I cannot fail, listening every moment to the Spirit's

---

[46] R. Kelso Carter (1886). Ephesians 6:14-17. Hymn Site.com. In *The United Methodist Hymnal*. Book of United Methodist Worship. Copyright © 1989 The United Methodist Publishing House. p. 374

call, resting in my Savior as my all in all—standing on the promises of God.

Relevant to the elderly is the promise in Isaiah 46:3–5, which says, "Listen to me, you descendants of Jacob, all the remnant of the people of Israel, you whom I have upheld since your birth, and have carried since you were born. Even to your old age and gray hairs I am he. I am he who will sustain you. I have made you and I will carry you; I will sustain you and I will rescue you." Other encouraging promises about the elderly include the following:

- Psalm 30:1-5: "I will exalt you, Lord, for you lifted me out of the depths and did not let my enemies gloat over me. Lord my God, I called to you for help, and you healed me. You, Lord, brought me up from the realm of the dead; you spared me from going down to the pit. Sing the praises of the Lord, you his faithful people; praise his holy name. For his anger lasts only a moment, but has favor lasts a lifetime; weeping may stay for the night, but rejoicing comes in the morning."

- Psalm 103:1-5: "Bless the Lord, O my soul, and all that is in me, bless his holy name. Bless the Lord, O my soul, and do not forget all his benefits- who forgives all your iniquity, who heals all your diseases, who redeems your life from the Pit, who crowns you with steadfast love and mercy, who satisfies you with good as long as you live so that your youth is renewed like the eagle's."

- Ruth 4:15: "He will renew your life and sustain you in your old age."

For the youthful we have the following promises about renewal of energy:

- Psalm 103:1–5: "Bless the Lord, O my soul, and all that is within me, bless his holy name, which satisfies you with good as long as you live so that your youth is renewed like the eagles."

- Isaiah 40:29–31: "He gives power to the faint, and strengthens the powerless. Even youths will faint and be weary. And the young will fall exhausted;

but those who wait for the Lord will renew their strength, they shall mount up with wings like eagles, they shall run and not be weary. They shall walk and not faint." The eagle soars rather than flies. It does not move its wings when it finds a current that moves it.

The promises of beauty, strength, and rescue are in the following illustration:

- Isaiah 35:2–4: " …it will burst into bloom; it will rejoice greatly and shout for joy. The glory of Lebanon will be given to it, the splendor of Carmel and Sharon; they will see the glory of the LORD, the splendor of our God. Strengthen the feeble hands, steady the knees that give way; say to those with fearful hearts, 'Be strong, do not fear; your God will come, he will come with vengeance; with divine retribution he will come to save you.'" (*NRSV* here.)

A great promise is found in Lamentations 3:22–23: "Because of the LORD's great love we are not consumed, for his compassions never fail. They are new every morning; great is your faithfulness." The steadfast love of the Lord never ceases. His mercies (goodness) never come to an end. A familiar hymn, "Great Is Thy Faithfulness,"[47] assures us: "Morning by morning new mercies I see. All I have needed thy hand hath provided. Great is thy faithfulness! Lord, unto me." Therefore, "Sing the praises of the Lord, you his faithful people; praise his holy name. For his anger lasts only a moment, but his favor lasts a lifetime: weeping may stay for the night, but rejoicing comes in the morning (Psalm 30:4-5)."

The promises for those of all ages are in Joshua 1:5-9 *(NRSV)*:

> No one shall be able to stand against you all the days of your life. As I was with Moses, so I will be with you; I will not fail you or forsake you. Be strong and courageous; for you shall put this people in possession of the land that I swore to their ancestors to give them.

---

[47] Thomas O. Chisholm, "Great Is Thy Faithfulness," in *Songs of Salvation* (1923). Text and music copyright © 1923, renewal 1951, Hope Publishing Co.

Only be strong and very courageous, being careful to act in accordance with all the law that my servant Moses commanded you; do not turn from it to the right hand or to the left, so that you may be successful wherever you go. This book of the law shall not depart out of your mouth; you shall meditate on it day and night, so that you may be careful to act in accordance with all that is written in it. For then you shall make your way prosperous, and then you shall be successful. I hereby command you: Be strong and courageous; do not be frightened or dismayed, for the LORD your God is with you wherever you go.

Remember that the personal presence of God's enduring love is greater than life and death. Promises give great hope, comfort, and instructions for being renewed day by day. Stand on the promises!

- Romans 8:28: "And we know that in all things God works for the good of those who love him, who have been called according to his purpose."

- Isaiah 58:9b-11: "'If you do away with…malicious talk and spend yourselves in behalf of the hungry…, your night will become like the noonday. The Lord will guide you always; he will satisfy your needs…and strengthen your frame. You will be like a well-watered garden, like a spring whose waters never fail.'"

- Matthew 6:33: "But seek first his kingdom and his righteousness, and all these things will be added unto you."

- Isaiah 42:6: "'I, the Lord, have called you in righteousness; I will take hold of your hand. I will keep you and will make you to be… a light….'"

- Matthew 7:7: "Ask and it will be given to you; seek and you will find; knock and the door will be opened for you."

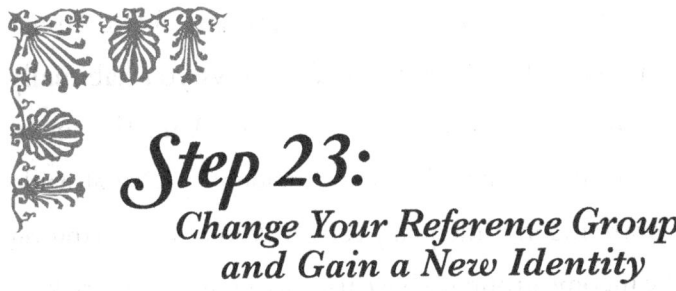

Step 23:
Change Your Reference Group and Gain a New Identity

You might have an identity crisis if you experience confusion as to who you are internally or externally. You become uncertain about what people think you can contribute, which groups accept you, or with whom you identify. Any identity crisis can occur independently of a need to change. It can relate to employment, loss of contributions from talent, loss of physical strength, alterations in family status, illness, or old age. When your life revolves solely around a person, job, house, or something else and it is lost or betrayed, you may feel devastated and rejected. But if your life revolves around Jesus Christ, you can move forward and count the loss as gain in being victorious with Him and His purposes. You may see Christ in others and respond victoriously.

Change friends or associates if the current ones are a

barrier to renewal, healing, and springing forth. Attend other churches. Switch the TV shows you habitually watch. Avoid certain advertisements. Vary the socio-economic group with whom you identify. Our attitude toward income adequacy can be altered with changing the income group we have used as a measuring stick.

Adopt the self-identity that you are a citizen in the kingdom of God. Become strengthened daily by basing your attitude and decisions on this self-concept and self-worth.

Die to the confusion and conflict of competing voices. Rise to see Christ as our measuring stick, our purpose, and our identity. Turn to Scripture and seek the Holy Spirit for direction in life. Wolgemuth[48] said it well: "Throughout Scripture, Jesus asks us to surrender our lives and our worldly thoughts, possessions, and desires, so that we might make room for the Holy Spirit to renew our minds and transform our lives. In a world where we are taught to use force to resolve conflict, where materialism rules and individualism is king, it is difficult to make that transition. However, if we surrender ourselves and leave everything be-

---

[48] Zack Wolgemuth, in Sunday morning church bulletin of Church of the Brethren, Lafayette, IN, February 7, 2010.

hind to follow Jesus, our lives are transformed and we experience the freedom of peace, simplicity, and togetherness."

A founder of the Brethren churches, Alexander Mack, wrote the following: "A soul which loves God finds anguish in this world. What it loves outside of Jesus is beset by terror and distress. Therefore Jesus calls us to it. Come, in me is joy and peace."

The competing voices are referred to in the song "Where Cross the Crowded Ways of Life."[49]

> Where cross the crowded ways of life,
> Where sound the cries of race and clan,
> Above the noise of selfish strife, We
> hear Thy voice, O Son of man.

"You are no longer foreigners and aliens, but fellow citizens with God's people" (Ephesians 2:19). Rejoice!

---

[49] Frank Mason North and William Gardiner, "Where Cross the Crowded Ways of Life," in *Sacred Melodies* (1850), published in *The Brethren Hymnal*. Copyright © 1951, House of the Church of the Brethren, Elgin, IL.

Step 24:
Use Light for Daily Guidance

Simple reminders, new disciplines, and symbols help us to be renewed daily. My collection of ceramic doves reminds me of love, the Holy Spirit, and peace. We see reminders every day of growing older and our deteriorating bodies, including our medicine, our calendar with doctors' appointments, cane, walker, wheel chair, and similar items. However, we also have other reminders of God's faithfulness. There are uplifting songs and slogans. Placing wall hangings, plaques, collections, and photographs throughout a house and yard helps guard against temptations to be forlorn and lose heart. For example, white doves remind me of the Holy Spirit, love, and peace. So I have collected them to view around the house and yard. Other reminders are angels, crosses, Bibles, lights, water, and a chair in a prayer garden.

A daily discipline that renews us is turning on a

light switch in our home and saying, "I turn on the Light of the world. I walk in the light. Jesus is the Light of the World and of my life. The Light pushes out the darkness and the evil ones who only walk in darkness. I come to the Light. Oh, help me, God."

Many verses proclaim the Light who loves us and the possibilities for healing, renewal, and giving hope to others:

- Job 33:28: "God has delivered me from going down to the pit and I shall live to enjoy the Light of Life."

- Psalm 13:3: "Look on me and answer, Lord my God. Give light to my eyes, or I will sleep in death."

- Psalm 43:3: "Send me your light and your faithful care, let them lead me; let them bring me to your holy mountain to the place where you dwell."

- Psalm 119:105: "Your word is a lamp for my feet, a light on my path."

- Matthew 4:15–16: "Land of Zebulon and land of Naphtali, the Way of the Sea, beyond the Jordan, Galilee of the Gentiles—the people living in darkness have seen a great light; on those living in the land of the shadow of death a light has dawned."

- John 8:12: "When Jesus spoke again to the people, he said, 'I am the light of the world. Whoever follows me will never walk in darkness, but will have the light of life.'"

- Matthew 5:16: "In the same way, let your light shine before others, that they may see your good deeds and glorify your Father in heaven."

- Isaiah 58:8–14: "Then your light will break forth like the dawn, and your healing will quickly appear; then your righteousness will go before you, and the glory of the Lord will be your rear guard. Then you will call, and the Lord will answer; you will cry for help, and he will say: 'Here am I.' then your light will rise in the darkness, and your night will become like the noonday. The LORD will guide you always; he will satisfy your needs in a sun-scorched land and will strengthen your frame. You will be like a well-watered garden, like a spring whose waters never fail. If you keep your feet from breaking the Sabbath and from doing as you please on my holy day, if you call the Sabbath a delight and the LORD's holy day honorable, and if you honor it by not going your own way and not doing as you please or speaking idle words, then you will find your joy in the LORD, For the mouth of the LORD has spoken."[50]

An appropriate song to share the Light all day long is "Christian, Let Your Burning Light."[51]

> Christian [your name], let your burning light shine on all with luster bright. Let your words and deeds be pure. All for Christ you must endure.

---

[50] This Scripture was a theme for the National Older Adult Conference, 2013, at Lake Junaluska, NC.

[51] E. G. Coleman, "Christian, Let Your Burning Light" (1898), in *Gospel Songs and Hymns No. 1* (1899).

[Refrain:] Christian, let your light shine all along the way. You may guide a wanderer to eternal day. You may save from endless night if you let your lamp burn bright.

As you journey here below shed a ray where're you go. Find in this your pure delight, let your light shine clear and bright. (Refrain)

That your light may guide you through, brightly let it shine anew. Keep up courage—never fail till you're safe within the vail. (Refrain)

An African-American spiritual, "This Little Light of Mine,"[52] could be sung all day:

This little light of mine, I'm goin'-a let it shine, this little light of mine, I'm

---

[52] "This Little Light of Mine" (music African-American), adapted by William F. Smith (1987). Music adaptation copyright © 1989 The United Methodist Publishing House.

goin'-a let it shine. This little light of mine, I'm goin'-a let it shine, let it shine, let it shine, let it shine.

Everywhere I go …

All through the night …

We can choose between the prevailing culture of death/killing/violence and of the culture of life/light. The culture of life is another way of saying The Kingdom or Reign of God with light, love, hope, joy and peace. Choose life! Be a light!

The Light is in us—even in the midst of darkness, fear, suffering, persecution, and despair, as well as in joyous celebrations. Rejoice!

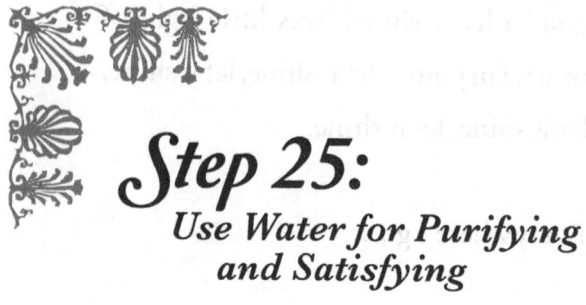

Step 25:
Use Water for Purifying and Satisfying

Each day when drinking water, we can remind ourselves also to drink the living water that satisfies. Jesus Christ is the Living Water. When washing hands, be cleansed of the impurities and renewed every time, every day. The title for Jesus used here—the Living Water—alludes to the spiritual healing and renewal from the True Source.

Illustrations are found in Scriptures about using the water for renewal and cleansing:

- John 4:10–13: "Jesus answered her, 'If you knew the gift of God and who it is that asks you for a drink, you would have asked him and he would have given you living water.' 'Sir,' the woman said, 'You have nothing to draw with and the well is deep. Where can you get this living water?

Are you greater than our father Jacob, who gave us the well and drank from it himself, as did also his sons and his livestock?' Jesus answered, 'Everyone who drinks this water will be thirsty again, but whoever drinks the water I give them will never thirst. Indeed, the water I give them will become in them a spring of water welling up to eternal life.' The woman said to him, 'Sir, give me this water so that I won't get thirsty and have to keep coming here to draw water.'"

- Psalm 36:8-10 *(NRSV)*; "They feast on the abundance of your house, and you give them drink from the river of your delights. For with you is the fountain of life; in your light we see light. O continue your steadfast love to those who know you, and your salvation to the upright of heart!"

- Jeremiah 17:13: "O Lord, the hope of Israel, all who forsake you will be put to shame. Those who turn away from you will be written in the dust because they have forsaken the Lord, the spring of living water."

As daily we wash ourselves, we are reminded of what Jesus said in Matthew 23:25–28: "Woe to you, teachers of the law and Pharisees, you hypocrites! You clean the outside of the cup and dish, but inside they are full of greed and self-indulgence. Blind Pharisee! First clean the inside of the cup and dish, and then the outside also will be clean. Woe to you, teachers of the law and Pharisees, you hypocrites! You are like whitewashed tombs, which look beautiful on the outside of the cup and dish but on the inside are full of dead men's bones and everything unclean. In the same way, on the outside you appear to people as righteous but on the inside you are full of hypocrisy and wickedness."

A song for cleansing and for social justice is "O Healing River."[53]

> O healing river, send down your waters,
> send down your waters upon this land.
> O healing river, send down your waters,
> and wash the blood from off the sand.

---

[53] "O Healing River" (text: anonymous; music: traditional hymn melody), in *Hymnal: A Worship Book*. Copyright © 1992, Brethren Press, Elgin, IL. All rights reserved.

Consider a poem I wrote, entitled "A Tree by Living Water." It draws from the following passages: Psalm 1; Jeremiah 2:12–14; John 4:10, 13; 7:38; Matthew 10:40–42.

> A tree fed by Living Water,
> A tree producing fruit,
> A tree living forever,
> That is what I want to be.
>
> A tree that does not wither,
> A tree planted with deep roots,
> A tree that smiles to everyone,
> That is what I want to be.
>
> Living Water from Christ's Spirit,
> Quenching thirst for me.
> Drinking the Water serves
> WWW World Wide Web.
>
> W for God's Word
> W for God's works
> W for God's world
> Surrounded by loving people.

Step 26:
Grow with Suffering

Patience with ourselves is necessary in order to grow and to receive peace and joy when we are really hurting. We can exercise patience as time passes and we seek progress in being healed. We can show patience with others helping us; and patience with God if we are not healed but rather cured. Cured means having contentment and peace with our situation although we are not healed. And there is our patience with God as we pray for healing but understand He might give us the ultimate cure, which is calling us home to Himself.

If we are hurting too much to pray, we can remember that the Spirit intercedes for us. Romans 8:26 says, "In the same way, the Spirit helps us in our weakness. We do not know what we ought to pray for, but the Spirit himself intercedes for us through wordless groans."

On this topic, it is worth repeating 2 Corinthians 4:17–18, from this book's theme, mentioned at the start: "For this slight momentarily affliction is preparing for an eternal weight of glory beyond all measure, because we look not at what can be seen but what cannot be seen; for what can be seen is temporary, but what cannot be seen is eternal." The following are some other thoughts on suffering:

1. Suffering is an experience that allows us to see God's holy presence and to depend more and more on Him. Some report they felt closer to God during their suffering than at other times.

2. Suffering helps us realize God's graces. Saint Paul prayed three times to have the thorn removed from his side. God said, "My grace is sufficient for you." Grace is all the wonderful blessings, comforts, gifts, and provisions that God has bestowed on us now or will in the future—making the pains and ailments a minor disturbance.

3. Let us be thankful that we can share in the suffering of Jesus. We worship a suffering Savior.

4. Temporal pain is minuscule compared to the glory, riches, and other gifts that we will experience in eternal life.

5. Suffering crosses over to the joy of the Lord who is our strength. (Nehemiah 8:10b)

6. We can feel honored, gratified, that Jesus invites us to join Him in the suffering of His being on the cross, to share in His suffering.

7. Through suffering we are purified, made refined—as gold. "Suffering builds character and character builds hope" (Romans 5:3-5).

8. We can help others when they suffer. We understand what they are dealing with—and we are able to console them, to pray with and for them. When someone tells us a concern for prayer, rather than saying "I will pray for you," stop at that moment and pray with the person on the spot.

9. We read in 2 Corinthians 1:3–7: "Praise be to the God and Father of our Lord Jesus Christ,

the Father of compassion and the God of all comfort, who comforts us in all our troubles [afflictions], so that we can comfort [encourage] those in any trouble with the comfort we ourselves receive from God. For just as we share abundantly in the sufferings of Christ, so also our comfort [encouragement] abounds through Christ. If we are distressed, it is for your comfort and salvation; if we are comforted [encouraged], it is for your comfort [encouragement], which produces in you patient endurance of the same sufferings we suffer. And our hope for you is firm, because we know that just as you share in our sufferings, so also you share in our comfort [encouragement]."

A summary of why grief, persecution, and suffering still occur after prayer is in 1 Peter 1:6–7: "In all this you greatly rejoice, though now for a little while you may have had to suffer grief in all kinds of trials. These have come so that the proven genuineness of your faith—of greater worth than gold, which perishes even though refined by fire—may result in praise, glory and honor when Jesus Christ is revealed."

Suffering in old age is recorded in 1 Kings 15:23: "As for all the other events of Asa's reign, all his achievements, all he did and the cities he built, are they not written in the book of the annals of the kings of Judah? In his old age, however, his feet became diseased. Then Asa rested with his ancestors and was buried with them in the city of his father David."

God's returning to help the elderly with problems or suffering is reiterated in Zechariah 8:3–5: "This is what the LORD says: 'I will return to Zion and dwell in Jerusalem. Then Jerusalem will be called the Faithful City, and the mountain of the LORD Almighty will be called the Holy Mountain.' This is what the LORD Almighty says: 'Once again men and women of ripe old age will sit in the streets of Jerusalem, each of them with cane in hand because of their age. The city streets will be filled with boys and girls playing there.'"

A friend said, "While I don't believe God sends pain and suffering (that's just part of the fallen world), He does expect His children to handle such things in a different manner than the rest of the society. In suffering, our faith can shine through and be a stronger witness than anything we can say. No matter how horrible our circumstances, it cannot compare to the pain and agony of Jesus giving His life for us."

"Come, Ye Disconsolate"[54] is a comfort song: "Come ye disconsolate, where'er ye languish, Come to the mercy seat, fervently kneel; Here bring your wounded hearts, here tell your anguish; Each has no sorrows that Heaven cannot heal."

An African song, "In Your Sickness,"[55] is a promise. "In your sickness, your suff'rings, your trials, and pains, he is with you all the time. Persecution, temptations, and loneliness, he is with you all the time."

Another promise is worth repeating: "The Lord is close to the brokenhearted and saves those who are crushed in spirit (Psalm 34:18)."

---

[54] Thomas Moore and Samuel Webbe, "Come, Ye Disconsolate," in *The Brethren Hymnal*. Copyright © 1951, House of the Church of the Brethren, Elgin, IL.

[55] "In Your Sickness," adapted from lyrics by Twi, in *Asempa Hymns*. Music: Ghanaian melody, from *Ghana Praise*. Text and music copyright © Asempa Publishers.

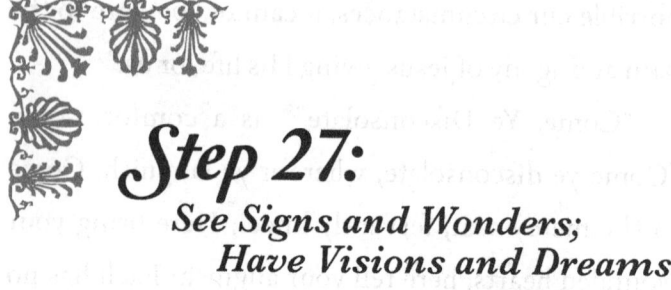

Step 27:
See Signs and Wonders; Have Visions and Dreams

Rather than seeing corruption wherever we look (and it is there), ask "Where have I seen God's hand moving today?" We can see God's hand in people's decisions and programs, their smiles, their help, in nature, in turns of events, and victories.

Rather than ending the day by seeing or hearing the broadcast news of corruption, sin, crime, war, violence, selfishness, and greed, we can review the *good news* of the Gospels. This will renew and heal us rather than discourage and add more anxiety.

Difficulty involving forgiveness is sometimes resolved through visions. Examples of forgiveness through visions include the following: A woman who lost her baby saw Jesus carrying her baby in His arms by the seashore, and she was comforted. A famous songwriter saw his mean father asking for forgiveness, and he forgave his father.

Visions also can build people up. A pastor saw the lame young girl in his congregation dancing in heaven, and he told her about it. A soldier saw Jesus on the cross in the battlefield, and he changed his mission.

As we grow older or have a major loss, let not our hearts become more hardened, but wiser instead. Otherwise, we risk becoming blind to the signs and wonders of God, skeptical of intervention, and less alert to see where God's hand is moving. We may increasingly think we cannot do something because of our health or other limitations. We may lose our confidence or deem ourselves inadequate. We fail to see many *delights* God has given, because we are stuck on ourselves and our problems.

Many people do not understand "signs and wonders" as related to healing and renewal. Illustrations in the Scriptures shed some light:

- Daniel 4:3: "How great are his signs, how mighty his wonders! His kingdom is an everlasting kingdom, and his sovereignty is from generation to generation." (*NRSV* is used throughout Step 27.)

- Daniel 6:27: "He delivers and rescues, he works signs and wonders in heaven and on earth; for he has saved Daniel from the power of the lions."

- Acts 7:36: "He led them out, having performed wonders and signs in Egypt, at the Red Sea, and in the wilderness for forty years."

Awareness of signs and wonders contributes to healing and renewal. Examples include the following:

- Jeremiah 32:20: "You showed signs and wonders in the land of Egypt, and to this day in Israel and among all humankind, and have made yourself a name that continues to this very day."

- Acts 2:22: "You that are Israelites, listen to what I have to say: 'Jesus of Nazareth, a man attested to you by God with deeds of power, wonders, and signs that God did through him among you, you yourselves know.'"

- Acts 2:43: "Awe came upon everyone, because many wonders and signs were shown by the apostles."

- Acts 4:30: "While you stretch out your hand to heal, signs and wonders are performed through the name of your holy servant Jesus."

- Acts 5:12: "Now many signs and wonders were done among the people through the apostles. And they were all together in Solomon's Portico."

- Acts 6:8: "Stephen, full of grace and power, did great wonders and signs among the people."

- Acts 14:3: "So they remained for a long time, speaking boldly for the Lord, who testified to the word of his grace by granting signs and wonders to be done through them."

- Acts 15:12: "The whole assembly kept silence, and listened to Barnabas and Paul as they told of all the signs and wonders that God had done through them among the Gentiles."

- Romans 15:19: "By the power of signs and wonders, by the power of the Spirit of God, so that from Jerusalem and as far around as Illyricum I have fully proclaimed the good news of Christ."

- Hebrews 2:4: " ...God added his testimony by signs and wonders and various miracles, and by gifts of the Holy Spirit, distributed according to his will."

Our vision can be voiced in "Be Thou My Vision."[56]

> Be thou my vision, O Lord of my heart; naught be all else to me save that thou art. Thou my best thought, by day or by night, waking or sleeping, thy presence my light.

---

[56] "Be Thou My Vision (orig. ancient Irish, "*Rob tu mo bhoile, a Comdi cride*"), trans. Mary Elizabeth Byrne in *Erin, Vol. 2* (1905); music: Irish melody, in *Old Irish Folk Music and Songs* (1909); harmonized by Martin Shaw, in *Enlarged Songs of Praise* (1931), alt. harmonization copyright © Oxford University Press, London.

Step 28:
Sing, Whistle, Play an Instrument, or Hum in Concert with the Spirit
(Outwardly or Inwardly)

Music heals and revives our spirit. I have heard that Martin Luther said, "He who sings prays twice." Beyond praying and breathing, we can sing, hum, or whistle, which brings out our spiritual nature, improving our physical condition. Music soothes and allays our fears, anxieties, loneliness, and the stress of weaknesses, unbelief, and calamities. Music connects us to the Spiritual.

Just playing a few notes on an instrument can renew our spirit. The most beautiful music for renewal and healing is your own voice, singing made-up tunes and words for your renewal and healing. Simply sing, or try drumming with a wooden spoon beating a pan.

Scripture in Ephesians 5:18–20 tells us, "Do not

get drunk on wine, which leads to debauchery. Instead, be filled with the Spirit, speaking to one another with psalms, hymns, and songs from the Spirit. Sing and make music from your heart to the Lord, always giving thanks to God the Father for everything, in the name of our Lord Jesus Christ." This may be too much when we are really hurting. Take time to grieve and pray that this step will be possible eventually with the Spirit praying for us.

In the spiritual experience of music, we can more readily receive the Spirit, who brings renewal. Sing or listen to music that touches the heart or spirit. A famous hymn with the theme of springing forth is "Glorious Things of Thee are Spoken." The words by John Newton were set to Franz Haydn's music in 1802: "See, the streams of living waters springing from eternal love, will supply they sons and daughters, and all fear of want remove. Who can faint while such a river ever flows, their thirst t'assuage – grace, which like the Lord the giver, never fails from age to age?"

Music is reported in Psalm 150:1-5: "Praise the Lord. Praise God in his sanctuary; praise him in his mighty heavens. Praise him for his acts of power; praise him for his surpassing greatness. Praise him with the sounding of the trumpet, praise him with the harp and lyre, praise him with timbrel and dancing, praise him with the strings and pipe, praise him with the clash of cymbals, praise him with resounding cymbals."

- Exodus 15:20-21: "Then Miriam the prophetess, Aron's sister, took a tambourine in her hand, and all the women followed her, with tambourines and dancing. Miriam sang to them: 'Sing to the Lord, for he is highly exalted.'"

- 1 Chronicles 16:9-10 "Sing to him, sing praise to him; tell of his wonderful acts. Glory in his holy name; let the hearts of those who seek the Lord rejoice."

- Psalm 28:6-7 "Praise be to the Lord, for he has heard my cry for mercy. The Lord is my strength and my shield; my heart trusts in him, and I am helped. My heart leaps for joy and I will give thanks to him in song."

Another renewal song is "Jesus, Draw Me Ever Nearer."[57]

> Jesus, draw me ever nearer as I labor through the Storm. You have called me to this passage, and I'll follow though I'm worn. May this journey bring a blessing, may I rise on wings of faith; and at the end of my heart's testing, with Your likeness let me wake.

Listen to great music, sing, hum, whistle, play music, and dance. Spring forth with a joyful heart and a renewed mind!

---

[57] Margaret Becker and Keith Getty, "Jesus, Draw Me Ever Nearer." Copyright © 2002, Modern Music.

Step 29:
Share Wisdom, Skills, Experience, and Love

Sharing renews us as well as the recipients. We have skills, experiences, attitudes, and love that we can share with others who greatly need the benefit of those gifts. We can share words of kindness and appreciation to service workers, for example, and to others regardless of our changing roles, ailing health, weak bodies, and feelings of inadequacy or dependence.

Wisdom to share comes in various ways. A search of Scripture reveals some ways:

- Ecclesiastes 2:26: "To the person who pleases him, God gives wisdom, knowledge and happiness, but to the sinner he gives the task of gathering and storing up wealth to hand it over to the one who pleases God."

- James 1:5–8: "If any of you lacks wisdom, you should ask God, who gives generously to all without finding fault, and it will be given to you. But when you ask, you must believe and not doubt, because the one who doubts is like a wave of the sea, blown and tossed by the wind. That person should not expect to receive anything from the Lord. Such a person is double-minded and unstable in all they do [vacillating between fear and faith]."

- 2 Chronicles 1:11–12: "God said to Solomon, 'Since this is your heart's desire and you have not asked for wealth, possessions or honor, nor for the death of your enemies, and since you have not asked for a long life but for wisdom and knowledge to govern my people over whom I have made you king, therefore wisdom and knowledge will be given you. And I will also give you wealth, possessions and honor, such as no king who was before you ever had and none after you will have.'"

Evidence of wisdom is in these verses:

- James 3:13: "Who is wise and understanding among you? Let them show it by their good life, by deeds done in the humility that comes from wisdom." This is sharing our love.

- Job 32:7-8: "I thought, 'Age should speak; advanced years should teach wisdom. But it is the Spirit in a man, the breath of the Almighty, that gives understanding.'"

In Scripture we read of the reputation of older people with wisdom:

- Job 32:9: "It is not only the old who are wise, not only the aged who understand what is right." Children, youth, young adults, etc. can share.

- Job 12:12: "Is not wisdom found among the aged? Does not long life bring understanding?"

- Psalm 90:12: "Teach us to number our days, that we may have a heart of wisdom."

- 1 Corinthians 2:6: "We do, however, speak a message of wisdom among the mature, but not the wisdom of this age or of the rulers of this age, who are coming to nothing."

We can share our wisdom with whomever and wherever. We are to have a spirit of boldness. Share willingly and freely your skills, experience, and love. The following are some relevant Scriptures:

- 1 Corinthians 2:13: "This is what we speak, not in words taught us by human wisdom but in words taught by the Spirit, explaining spiritual realities with Spirit-taught words."

- Colossians 1:9: "For this reason, since the day we heard about you, we have not stopped praying for you. We continually ask God to fill you with the knowledge of his will through all the wisdom and understanding that the Spirit gives." We pray that you are filled with love.

Renewal by sharing and the Holy Spirit is proclaimed in "There Is a Balm in Gilead."[58]

> There is a balm in Gilead to make the wounded whole; There is a balm in Gilead to heal the sinsick soul.
>
> Sometimes I feel discouraged, And think my work in vain, But then the Holy Spirit revives my soul again.
>
> If you can't preach like Peter, If you can't pray like Paul, Just tell the love of Jesus, and say He died for all.

Everyone has had experiences from which we can learn. Recognizing their wisdom and gifts is a way of sharing love. Do not let discrimination prevent sharing. Be bold!

---

[58] "There Is a Balm in Gilead" (African-American spiritual; no author; in public domain), published in *Hymns for the Family of God* (Nashville, TN: Paragon Associates). Copyright © 1976. International copyright secured. All rights reserved.

Step 30:
Look Up; Look Forward; Look Inward to Your Beautiful Self Who Has Survived and Overcome Obstacles; Look to God and to the Place God Has Prepared for You

The poem "My Name Is I Am" (Yahweh's name) by Helen Mellicoat[59] explains how we can look to God moment by moment:

> I was regretting the past and fearing the future.
> Suddenly my Lord was speaking:
> "My name is I AM."
> He paused. I waited. He continued.
> "When you live in the past
> with its mistakes and regrets, it is hard.

---

[59] Helen Mellicoat "My Name Is I Am," reprinted at http//www.inspiring-quotes-and-stories.com/my-name-is-i-am-html

> My name is not I WAS.
> When you live in the future,
> with its problems and fears, it is hard.
> I am not there.
> My name is not I WILL BE.
> When you live in this moment it is _not_ hard.
> I am here. My name is - I AM."

Every day we can declare, as said in Zephaniah 3:17, "We are God's delight. He delights in us." A daily discipline of renewal affirms this. Also, we must act in a way that brings delight to someone, helping the person to feel joyful and uplifted.

We have this exhortation and assurance from Zephaniah 3:16b–17 *(NKJV)*:

... let not your hands be weak. The Lord your God is in your midst, The Mighty One, will save; He will rejoice over you with gladness [He delights in you]. He will quiet [cover] you in His love, He will rejoice over you with singing.

Alternate translations of Zephaniah 3:17 give added meanings:

- *New Living Translation.* "For the Lord your God is living among you. He is a mighty savior. He will take delight in you with gladness. With his love, he will calm all your fears. He will rejoice over you with joyful songs."

- *Revised Standard Version Catholic Edition.* (This version includes the concept of *renewal*.) "The Lord, your God, is in your midst, a warrior who gives victory; he will rejoice over you with gladness, he will renew you in his love; he will exult over you with loud singing."

Singing a song is "In My Heart There Rings a Melody" by Elton M. Roth, 1934. "I have a song that Jesus gave me. It was sent from heaven above; There never was a sweeter melody, 'Tis a melody of love."

Our trust is shown in Psalm 37:3-4, 23-24, 27-28: "Trust in the Lord and do good; dwell in the land and enjoy safe pasture. Take delight in the Lord, and he will give you the desires of your heart. The Lord makes firm the steps of the one who delights in him; though he may stumble, he will not fall, for the Lord upholds him with his hand. Turn from evil and do good; then you will dwell in the land forever. For the Lord loves the just and will not forsake his faithful ones."

Furthermore, we can stand on the greatest promise, from John 14:1–3:

> Let not your heart be troubled; you believe in God, believe also in Me. In my Father's house there are many dwelling places. If it were not so, would I have told you that I go to prepare a place for you? And if I go and prepare a place for you, I will come again and will take you to myself, so that where I am, there you may be also.

Praise the Lord! What an assurance for the grand finale when we spring forth to the everlasting life! Meanwhile, the Living Presence is within us, giving us strength, love, joy, and peace, moment by moment.

Part II
Enlightenment, Edification, and Education

In preparing this book, I solicited essays to address the day-to-day issues common to those with affliction, loss, and aging. This part presents those essays as well as more of my writings. I invite you to consider these practical, educational, and inspirational writings for change and renewal. Equipping us for the journey is the technical, social, emotional, and spiritual advice from these real people with real experiences. Enriching ourselves daily by reading these and similar writings can help free the spirit to renew us, recover emotionally and physically, change our near environment, and hope by taking steps.

Disrupted by Life
Jason Willoughby[60]

Let us accept that interruptions are "normal" in life's journey. Jason Willoughby explains this in the following essay.

We all do it.

We all carry plans secretly in our minds of how we think life will go.

They are the unspoken expectations we have for events, for other people, for the future, and for ourselves.

But these plans are fragile.

They are so easily disrupted by events beyond our control. What's on paper becomes confetti and is blown to the wind. Just ask Congress.

---

[60] Written January 3, 2013, by Jason Willoughby, Pastor, Bethel Baptist Church in McMinnville, OR. E-mail: reachthecityministries@gmail.com; family e-mail: all4jesus@frontier.com; cell: 1-503-560-7923; address: 640 NW Brookview Court, McMinnville, OR 97128.

On December 5, my mom suffered a major stroke that left her with very limited speaking abilities. And my dad is showing signs of early dementia.

They are in their eighties. They are definitely acting their age. It was going to happen sooner or later. And yet …

I just spent the last eight days with them, assessing their home situation, making arrangements for many appointments, and advocating on their behalf with various agencies and bureaucracies.

Ugh!

I needed to be always on, always vigilant, always aware of medications not taken and things on the calendar but forgotten.

And it was a test of our family–old conflicts are always there to resurface and old wounds make hard things even harder. We are all under duress dealing with matters we'd rather not face.

None of this was in my plans. None of it was quite like I expected it to be.

I always thought my parents would be incapacitated or impaired–one at a time. I never thought my sister and I would be dealing with them both impaired at the same time.

I found myself not only working through my own grief, but this kind of life disruption means I am dealing with their grief, too. In some ways, I am now the parent and they are the children.

And that's weird—and sad. My mind tells me it's how life works. My heart protests against this reversal.

They needed vast amounts of compassion, patience, and understanding this past week. And will need much, much more in the coming months.

Thank God that He can give us such qualities when we need them most. It was refreshing to admit I'm an amateur, have never done this before, don't know what I'm doing, and have a lot to learn.

And then ask Him for help each day and actually be helped. Yes, disruptions have a way of scouring away any lingering pretensions of adequacy. And they also drive us to the grace of God.

Not only are my parents vulnerable right now, but so am I.

And that's good for our souls.

Grief in Seniors
Judy Hollandsworth[61]

Grief permeates heart, spirit, mind, and body. Regardless of whether the cause of grief is loss or changing circumstances, healing is possible. Recovery takes time and attention. The mistake is to try to ignore grief and find distractions rather than "licking one's wounds,"(although crying and pleading in prayer is important for awhile. Although people handle grief in different ways, remember that God is close to the brokenhearted and saves those crushed in spirit (Psalm 34:17–18). Take time to experience the misery and affliction—temporarily—as it leads to renewal. Eventually the mourning leads to joy in the morning. (See Esther 9:22) Jesus promised He would

---

[61] Judy Hollandsworth is a sacred dancer, choreographer, worship leader, and writer. She is a licensed minister in the Church of the Brethren. She is owner of Worship Dance and is treasurer and a founding member of Women of Worship (WOW), a non-denominational, international, multi-racial sacred dance group, founded in 2001. She is co-resources chair for the international Sacred Dance Guild.

send a counselor, a comforter. A present help in sorrow is found in reading the Psalms. They contain records of crying out, complaining, and anguish. The shadows of death and despair will disappear with the Light eternal.

In the following brief essay, Judy Hollandsworth—a worship leader and sacred dancer—writes about grief. She administered interviews.

A seminar in 2013 led by David Kessler, a protégé of Elizabeth Kubler-Ross, used these concepts[62]:

1. Grief is as "miraculous as a wound healing."
2. Grief ultimately shapes our growth.
3. We don't run from grief itself but from the pain of loss.
4. Our souls are broken when we don't allow grief to happen.

The folks at the Family Caregiver Alliance[63] say the following:

---

[62] Seminar in 2013 led by David Kessler.

[63] Family Caregiver Alliance has services available in many cities in the United States; http://www.caregiver.org/jsp/content_node.jsp?nodeid=404.

Those impacted by sudden loss do not have the luxury of preparation; a car accident, heart attack, or some other natural/unnatural cause of death that is quick and strikes without warning means that the family and friends are left to grieve without having closure.

People who lose a loved one suddenly are often plagued by guilt of a different kind: "I didn't get to say goodbye!" or "The last thing I said to her was something harmful/mean!" or "I never told him how much I loved him." Unresolved issues like these can haunt the living and impede their ability to move up and out of their grief if they don't seek appropriate help.

Suicide is an especially difficult type of sudden loss because it leaves family and friends wishing they could have seen the signs and prevented such a heartbreaking end. After a suicide, loved ones are tormented by so many questions that sadly will remain unanswered.

Grief in seniors is more intense because they have already had many losses. They have lost a job, or their children are no longer at home, or perhaps they have lost a child or a child has not lived up to their expectations. Almost certainly they have lost their parents. In fact, older adults' losses occur in a short period of time and they are of many and different kinds. Examples of loss include losing independence, physical strength, health, and the ability to remember.

Minor losses can bring back feelings from a greater loss. LQWilliams[64] tells us that "losses can have multiple ramifications, including psychological, social, and physical. For example, the loss of a driver's license due to physical or mental limitations can affect self-esteem, independence, and a person's sense of responsibility. As with this example, there are many losses that have

---

[64] LQWilliams, "Coping with Loss and Grief for Seniors," updated December 9, 2012, http://www.hubpages.com/hub/Coping-with-Loss-and-Grief-for-Seniors. LQWilliams is a master's level social worker with more than fifteen years of therapeutic services with child protective services, mental health support services, and medical social work.

a broader symbolic meaning and multiple losses can severely strain a person's ability to cope."

There is also a great possibility of depression, but grief and depression are a lot alike, making it difficult to tell one from the other. LQWilliams says, "Depression affects approximately 6 million Americans age 65 and older. Of these, only about 10% receive treatment." The danger in this is suicide. LQWilliams adds, "The suicide rate for elders 80 to 85 is more than twice that of the general population."

LQWilliams advises as follows:

> There are several ways to look at the grief process. Generally speaking, a grieving person must accomplish four tasks in order to regain balance in life:
>
> 1. Accept the reality of the loss
> 2. Experience the pain of grief
> 3. Adjust to the changes
> 4. Withdraw emotional energy from what was lost and reinvest it in people and/or other activities[65]

---

[65] Ibid.

I conducted personal interviews to determine the actual experience of loss in seniors. The first interview was with someone who had lost her husband very suddenly but fortunately had some pastoral help. The woman, Dorothy,[66] did not attend a group, but personal counseling with her pastor helped her tremendously. At the first discussion she described this shock and the effect it had on her boys. The older one thought he needed to be the man now. The five-year-old would ask to see Daddy, but what he actually wanted was to visit the grave. She summarized her pastor's advice as follows: "Write a letter to the deceased loved one. Have an ongoing journal. Remember that God's love and power will be sufficient. Begin to get on with living. These will help with healing."

Based on some pastoral counseling materials that her pastor sent to her, Dorothy included the following advice:

> The Lord will give you the strength to
> go through this because you can't do
> it alone. God's love and power will be

---

[66] Dorothy Pope, Buck Creek Church of the Brethren, Mooreland, IN.

sufficient. Life will never be the same again, but you won't always feel like this—like you do right now. There is no typical grief cycle. You began to heal and get back into living but you still remember that person, son, daughter, spouse, or whomever.

In the days, weeks, months, years following a son's death, I have put one foot in front of the other and carried on the best that you can. If someone asked me how I coped with losing a child, the answer is you don't. You just go on—there is no other choice. There is a part of me missing and always will be. My son is never out of my mind and I still miss him.

I can do the hard things ... I've walked the valley of death's shadow, so deep and dark that I could barely breathe. And I've questioned everything that I believe. But even in the great darkness a comfort and hope comes breaking

> through. As I can say in life or death, "God, we belong to you."
>
> Endurance is not just the ability to bear a hard thing, but to turn it into glory. You can kill yourself either literally or emotionally by crawling into bed and never getting out. Or you can put one foot in front of the other and take baby steps forward.

Steps toward recovery may not continue in the same order for everyone, because everyone's timetable is different. Some experience depression and even suicidal thoughts. Be sure to seek help from your doctor and some form of counseling when these occur.

The pastor also shared with Dorothy a list of experiences common to people who are going through grief,[67] as follows:

1. Shock—denial
2. Emotional release

---

[67] Granger E. Westburg, *Good Grief* (Minneapolis, MN: Fortress Press). Copyright © 1971.

3. Expression and isolation of grief; "This too shall pass."
4. Physical symptoms
5. Guilt—true or false
6. Panic or obsession about the loss
7. Hostility (anger and anxiety)
8. Idealizations of the past—unacceptable changes
9. Struggle for new patterns of living
10. Reaffirmation of reality

The experiences of people going through the grief process show us that a return to some kind of routine is essential to recovery from grief. It doesn't mean that the deceased person is no longer remembered or that grief is over, but it does mean that the person grieving begins the healing process.

A woman recounted the shock of her grandson's death. He was killed in a traffic accident, so it was a big shock. The woman, Orlynn,[68] was in the shower at the YMCA. The people at the Y gave her a bottle of water and drove her to her apartment, and then she drove

---

[68] Orlynn Houser, Buck Creek Church of the Brethren, Mooreland, IN.

herself to the home where the family was gathered in mourning. The deceased grandson's sister was not doing well at all, because their mother (the woman's daughter) had died in a traffic accident several years earlier. This woman's advice was to get back to things you normally do as soon as possible. She had no choice after her daughter's accident but to go back to work. After her husband died, she went back to work after two or three weeks.

Grief after Long Caregiving
Judy Hollandsworth

Grief after a long period of giving care to a loved one is different from the shock of sudden death, because there has been plenty of time to do some of the things that both people enjoy. Also, usually the grieving has started even before the ailing person has died. The folks at the Family Caregiver Alliance[69] call this *anticipatory grief* and describe it as follows: "Anticipatory grief occurs when a loved one dies of a terminal or prolonged illness, like cancer or Alzheimer's. Family and friends in this case often feel guilty for hoping that death will come quickly if an illness/disease has caused great suffering, discomfort or diminished quality of life. While the loss is just as painful despite the fact that it was expected, loved ones in this scenario have the opportunity to identify and accommodate

---

[69] Family Caregiver Alliance is an agency available in many cities and on the Internet.

the final wishes of the dying person, say goodbyes, clear the air on any previous misunderstandings, and prepare emotionally for the separation."

I conducted personal interviews in 2013 to examine the experience of anticipatory grief. Most of these persons had an experience of anticipatory grief, but some had sudden-death grief, and a few had both. The following questions were given to the people several days or weeks before the interview, and then answers were obtained in the interview:

1. How did it feel when you were no longer a caregiver?
2. If it was sudden, how did you feel then?
3. How long did it take to return to some kind of routine?
4. What helped you recover?
5. What would you recommend for recovery?
6. What would you recommend to seniors who are suicidal? (Many are after the death of a spouse.)
7. Other comments?

Selected Responses to Interview Questions

Question 1: How did you feel?

"In my niece Kathy's case, we counted twenty years of caregiving. When her mother passed, she was still the caregiver of her dad, so it was mostly relief and sadness. When her dad passed away there was a sense of relief that he was no longer suffering but sadness in not hearing him speak with his long-deceased wife. He had talked to her in the early morning and Kathy could hear him through the baby monitor in her house next door. At that time she decided to turn it off, so he could have privacy. He confided to her that Mary's spirit came to him, rubbing his head, etc. Kathy later had to move because she couldn't stand to see their house occupied by others every day."

Other responses: "Free, then lonely, sense of not doing something that should be done; glad I did everything possible for them;" "lost;" "relief and sorrow for death;" and "what do I do now?" Carlene set her clock and checked on her husband every hour during the last six weeks, when the doctor said it would not be long now. She had to have sleeping pills afterwards for a while to get her sleep schedule back.

Question 3: How long before returning to routine?

"Back to my niece Kathy—her mother [Mary] was so tired from taking care of Grandmother Marie, helped her in the evening after work and finally hired help to care for her. Mary and George had about four good years of traveling around North Carolina and Virginia and enjoying activities at home, before Mary got cancer. Toward the end Mary told Kathy that she and George had always said, 'One day,' they would … and now there will be no more 'one days' to come. She urged Kathy not to put things off."

Other responses: After some deaths, Orlynn had to go back to work pretty quickly, so there was some sort of routine. Another interview had to help prepare for two more family funerals and a reunion, and still cared for a senior and a baby under a year old. Another interviewee said it took three months to establish a new routine, but after that she was able to go to the lake often. Another said it took three and a half years to get back into somewhat of a routine; another, at least a year.

Question 4: What helps recovery?

More from Kathy: What helped Kathy the most were photos, good memories. The holidays were hard, but the family lit Chinese lanterns and let them float up to heaven. Upgrading the old house where they moved was her therapy. But what helped the most was time and reconciling to the idea that we are born and raised in the church to live a certain way to prepare for heaven. Kathy said, "Yet as a society we fight so hard the 'going to heaven' part. Death is a natural part of the life cycle. We need to take care of ourselves with resting, reading and quiet times."

Kathy believes that her mother physically recovered but never mentally from Grandmother Marie's death. She fretted that she could have done more. Kathy and her husband agree that her dad George was lost. They had been married fifty-seven years. He had made heart-wrenching tapes as memorials to her mother, Mary. She could hardly listen to them.

Others responses: Orlynn believes that her church family, friends, and faith helped in recovery. Another interviewee agreed as to church support and family, and added "doing enjoyable things." Others suggested projects and church meetings, walking through a store just to get out of the house, and getting out to be with people.

Question 5: Recommendations for recovery.

Orlynn recommends getting back to a routine as soon as possible and making no big decisions for a year. She says, "And if you like gardening, do that as soon as you can."

Hospice's bereavement group is highly recommended by my niece, Kathy. She also was helped by a dream: Her mother was visiting her to let her see that she was alright. She also says talk about the deceased, make an effort to be involved in the world, stay involved with your church (or group) and your family, volunteer, and get a hobby.

Others recommend getting back to a routine as soon as possible, staying involved, not being alone much, going to a grief group, and not sitting at home.

Question 6: Recommendations for those who are suicidal.

One woman said, "My niece has experienced most everything. Her first husband's father committed suicide right before their wedding. They often wondered if it was because of the wedding. He told everyone he was getting married too, but of course he wasn't there." That interviewee also said, "Take every thought or expression about suicide very seriously and do whatever it takes to get help." Carlene said, "Count your blessings and rely on God. Most of all remember to take all thoughts or expressions of suicide very seriously."

In conclusion, remember to do things that you both enjoy, while you still are coherent or able. Take the advice of those who have experienced it.

Medicine Management
Marie Willoughby[70]

Here is a report about a couple who manage.

I asked my husband, "Which pills did you say? I can't find them for you. Yes, I've looked all over your *pharmacy*. Where on this table did you put them?"

Is this a common situation at your house, too?

---

[70] Marie Willoughby was born in Hershey, PA, in 1935. Her father was a farm hired hand and in the free ministry for the Koontz Church of the Brethren. Her mother was an elementary school teacher and principal. Marie graduated from Elizabethtown High School in 1953 (valedictorian) and from Elizabethtown College in 1957, then taught grade 5 and 6 in Elizabethtown Public School for two and a half years and grades 3–4 in Oak Lawn, IL, for one year. For twenty-five years she did substitute teaching for several school districts. Marie married Don Willoughby of Harrisonburg, PA, in Vienna, Austria, where he had completed two and a half years of Brethren Volunteer Service. When Don graduated from Elizabethtown College in 1960, they moved to Chicago, Illinois, where he attended Bethany Biblical Seminary, graduating in 1964. Don and Marie are the parents of six children and have one grandchild.

When my husband and I moved into our present apartment, we asked the maintenance crew to remove the closet doors so we could set up a card table inside that space. Well, the table fits almost all the way in. There's a folding chair beside it. As before we moved, the cloth on the table is the one my parents received as a wedding gift eighty years ago. The cloth is safe there. On the table is a multitude of vitamins, minerals, ointments, and prescription drugs. Each variety has its own place on the table, but you know how it is. Things move around. Or you run out.

My husband ordinarily handles this very well,

Besides raising a family and teaching school, Marie was active in her local church, teaching Sunday school, singing in and leading choirs, visiting, and editing the newsletter. She also worked in various capacities in the districts where they lived. She served as a district youth advisor, on the district Nurture Commission, as chair of the district board, on the district women's cabinet, as moderator of the District Conference (three times), and eventually served seven years as the (part-time) district executive in Michigan.

Retiring in February 2009, Marie and Don moved to the Timbercrest Senior Living Community in North Manchester, IN. Marie is currently president of the Koinonia Sunday School in the Manchester Church of the Brethren, is secretary for the Timbercrest Chapel Planning Committee, and prepares the one-page life story of new residents at Timbercrest.

entirely by himself. Every so often (as needed) he fills the pill strips with all the pills needed for a week—a little compartment for each day. He has three strips, which mean three weeks' worth of pills. In the mornings, at the breakfast table, he has to pick out the morning pills and then store the rest until bedtime. Now, I use two small strips. One for my morning pills and one for my bedtime pills. But then, I have to fill them *every* week! Not him! Why doesn't he get another strip and do this only once a month!

How is one supposed to keep track of all the pills? So many of them these days. And then with three or four different doctors doing the prescribing, it's a mess. And even more so when the dosage gets changed in the course of things. Who changed what, to what? Do I take just half a pill, or do I take one and a half? Do I do it every day, or every other day? I use a chart to keep track.

"What! You don't have a chart? Get with it, man. Write all this stuff down," I say to my husband.

"Yeah, sure," he says. "You only have three prescriptions; I have eight, plus the vitamins and calcium and TUMS and ... oh, it's too much!"

There are the eye drops, and the medicated

lotions ... And then there's the insulin that's not even on the table.

What a pain that is. He has to test his blood sugar every morning! At least it's not four times a day any more. But there are still four daily insulin injections. Each time, it requires getting the insulin out of the refrigerator, undoing the alcohol pad from its wrapping, drawing the right amount into the syringe, pulling up one or more shirts, rubbing the skin, injecting at the right place. Four times a day! I get tired of it. I really, really get tired of it.

I asked my husband, "What would happen if I just didn't do all this for you anymore? What would happen?"

He responded, "You'd be miserable, that's what."

I said, "I'm already miserable." I continued: "I know, but you are worth the effort. What can I do to be more helpful? I'm so glad that you can still do some of this yourself."

He said, "But the day is coming ..."

I replied, "Yeah, I know. I never wanted to be a nurse. Is this nursing? No, it's caregiving. And I care about you. I really do. When I need to, I'll prepare and administer your meds. You're worth it, and I love you. Stay with me."

Traveling
Marie Willoughby

Change of scenery—daily or occasionally—enhances renewal, healing, and hope. Travel can renew one's heart, mind, and spirit. Effective planning and management of travel prevents problems. Experiencing successful excursions will reduce the likelihood of slipping back into inactivity.

We're going away for the weekend, and we are looking forward to seeing the family. It never has been a *breeze* to just pack up and go. But as we get older, it takes quite a bit of planning. Making a list and checking it twice—or more.

The clothes part is easy. But always add at least one extra set of things, especially underwear. One never knows. Toiletries aren't too bad either. A kit is often all ready to go. And don't forget a flashlight. You might even want to take a plug-in night light (which is easy to forget to bring back again). [A charger for the cell phone is a must.]

It's the medicine tote bag that needs the most attention. Again, take no less than one extra day's worth of everything, and preferably more. Besides prescription meds, we include in the tote bag various other items a small lidless box for easy selection—things such as lotions, wipes, pain pills, insulin pens, three-by-five cards, writing pens, and nail clippers. This tote bag stays with us inside the car, not in the trunk or out of reach anywhere. Insulin that needs refrigeration goes into a small cooler with several cans of soft drinks. This, too, stays within reach. The first aid kit stays with us inside the car as well.

We also prepare a notebook—a very thorough notebook with plastic sleeves. This handy, dandy travel companion contains the following:

- our agenda, with times and places.

- telephone numbers for the whole family (even though the numbers are now in my cell phone).

- contact information for doctors, pastors, neighbors, and so on.

- maps; printed directions to locations we plan to visit; pictures from Google Maps.

- our "Final Wishes" or end-of-life documents (copies, of course).

- most important of all, several copies of lists of all of our medications (names of drugs, times of day to take them, doses, usage instructions) as well as contact information for all of our medical people (names, addresses, and telephone numbers).

As to the medical and drug information: We each have our own list. I don't think there's anywhere to get a description of how you can tell which pill is which. That would take a lot of space. But pharmacists and nurses know.

We carry several copies of these medication pages because they are handy to leave with anyone who needs to know, and this saves the person from having to write it all down immediately.

There's another list to check off before we leave our home. Unplug the computers and TVs, water the plants, arrange for the mail, close the windows, lock the doors ... These are good plans no matter what age you are.

When we were younger, we could start out at any time of day. But now the earlier the better. Well, not before eight or nine in the morning. We plan for a couple extra hours of travel time in order to take more and longer breaks—rest stops and meals usually. And we want time after arrival to rest up, with feet up, before doing anything else. It's also nice to do serendipitous things, like pull into an overlook and enjoy the scenery, or find a historic site and learn something, or look through a cemetery and make up stories.

If we are on our own, with more than a one-day journey, we will check into our hotel before supper ("dinner" to many). Then one of us will go out to find food and bring it back to the room. That's called dining in.

Sharing the driving is still possible for us. But this may not always be the case. We're aware that our traveling experiences will change as the years go on. And this may be coming sooner than we think or want. Already, the kids (in their fifties) are saying, "Can you come on your own? Or do you want someone to come and drive for you?" It's very nice of them to think of this and to offer. Distances and direction would make this kind of help a stretch for them, and for us. But we'll take them up on it—sometime.

We're taking a trip for the weekend. Is it worth it? Should we stay longer so as to make worthwhile all of the preparations? We did a three-week trip less than a year ago. It went well because we took plenty of time and enjoyed each day (each short day, that is). Never overload yourself. Say no often. Smile—everyone has a camera!

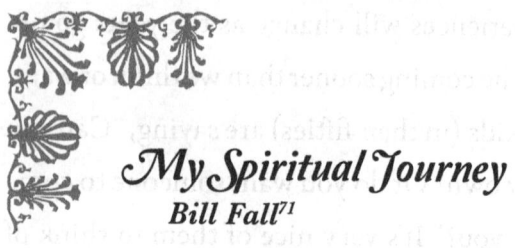

My Spiritual Journey
Bill Fall[71]

> I am absolutely convinced that nothing—nothing living or dead, angelic, or demonic, today or tomorrow, high or low, thinkable or unthinkable—absolutely nothing can get between us and God's love because of the way Jesus our Master has embraced us. (Romans 8:38–39 *MSG*)

Bill shares his journey of how he coped with loss and suffering, survived, and was renewed.

---

[71] Bill Fall was born in Abtington, Minnesota, in 1917. After graduation from high school, he was active in World War II. He served in the Korean conflict. He was an instructor at Purdue University in the Midwest Program on Airborne Television Instruction (MPATI), starting in 1960. He filled positions created by Purdue University after closure of MPATI until retirement. He is active in Covenant Church, West Lafayette, IN.

When first I was asked to prepare an essay for inclusion in this collection, I was a bit nonplussed. Nonetheless I agreed, albeit with more than a few reservations. Subsequently, as I pondered and prayed, it came to me! I could share some highlights of my spiritual journey. Few, if any of us, follow a well charted path through life, well marked and well lit. For most of us there are side roads, detours, rough pathways, steep hills with dangerous curves, and more than a few potholes along the way. All of us are sojourners. Each of us has many stories to tell about one's own wanderings.

In going through a review process in order to articulate facets of my pilgrimage, I am unable to point to a Damascus Road experience. In the main my journey has been of the deliberate, plodding kind, with plenty of desert experiences, but also with innumerable oases along the way where I found water and manna.

I am going to fast forward, skipping my growing up, World War II, the Korean affair, and other early stages of my journey. Suffice it to say the Holy Spirit was at work during those years and the sanctification process was underway, unbeknown to me.

In the mid-1970s I started journaling. I was drawn

into it because I needed to resolve issues about my mother's death and the settling of her estate. Today, journaling is a part of my life—since the death of Joyce, my wife, in 1989, it has been almost every day. It has been invaluable in the healing process, which, incidentally, goes on still. I confess to you: I am a wounded wanderer, and I will limp and ache for the rest of my life without her.

There is an entry that I would like to share with you, but space constraints overrule. It is now nearly thirty years after the fact. The following is a summary of the events the journal entry described. We were returning from a Purdue–Iowa football game with friends. Joyce and I got into a brouhaha about money she had inherited. She reflected as how she hankered after a new freezer. I didn't like the idea. We debated a bit—then argued—and finally, I, in my own inimitably sarcastic way, said, "Well, if you would just defrost the one we have we wouldn't need a new one!" Talk about deep freezes! The silence all across Illinois, including dinner in Peoria, was deafening. When we got home and walked into our bedroom, I was prompted to say something to the effect of defrosting the refrigerator and our lives. "No" was the immediate response.

I now know that the Holy Spirit prompts my comments—and puts me on my knees at bedside. I prayed to God with contrite heart for forgiveness, for healing, for Christ to be Lord of my life and Master of our marriage. I became aware that Joyce had joined me there on her knees, and she prayed as well. If any single significant thing happened to change our lives, that was it. It was the fountain of a succession of positives in our lives, the opening of a door to a new level of joy in our marriage.

Let me share one entry dated April 29, 1989, twenty days after Joyce's death:

> It's a different life, one which I certainly would not choose. We lived well together for forty-six years, one month and three days, five hours, and forty-four minutes. It wasn't all peaches and cream—neither one of us ever made any such claim. We recognized that we were individuals—we did have our moments, our differences of opinion—that's what made it go; we made allowances. As I look back on our life

together I can see the working of the Lord. He knew what he was doing when he put us together because we were sufficiently opposite that there was an attraction. Her strengths were my weaknesses, and my strengths were her weaknesses, and we functioned together as a team. That was exciting. I have to face the reality that this old horse is left in harness and she is out to pasture. It is not going to be an easy load to pull.

I get great comfort and great joy—and I am beginning to appreciate what it means to say "Rejoice in the Lord always, and again, I say, rejoice." Even in the face of a tragedy such as this, there is room and occasion for rejoicing. I rejoice at the impact Joyce made on countless lives. It is mind boggling to realize that she had a hand in changing people—was an instrument of the Holy Spirit. She didn't know this, didn't realize it at all—she wasn't even looking for it particularly. She just was. She was as close to being like a child of God as anyone I have ever known.

Critical to my spiritual formation was the ongoing and ever-challenging effort to adhere to the seven disciplines:

1. *The Discipline of Prayer.* To pray every day, preferably at the beginning of the day.

2. *The Discipline of Scripture.* To read reverently and thoughtfully, every day, a portion of Scripture, following a definite plan.

3. *The Discipline of Worship.* To share, at least once each week, in the public worship of God.

4. *The Discipline of Money.* To give a definite portion of my annual income to the promotion of Christ's cause.

5. *The Discipline of Time.* To use my time as a sacred gift, not to be wasted, striving to make my daily work, whatever it may be, a Christian vocation.

6. *The Discipline of Service.* To try, every day, to lift some human burden.

7. *The Discipline of Study.* To develop my mental powers by careful reading and study.

As I have tried to live out the disciplines, I have become aware that God responds. In my own faulted way I try to live with those disciplines. Sometimes I get careless and forget one or more in a given day, or even days, but in general these have become my guidelines.

I am convinced that God has a sense of humor. There are more reasons for that conviction than there is space remaining to relate them, but one incident may suffice to give you an idea of the way God's Holy Spirit works. We moved to West Lafayette in 1960 so I could take a job with Purdue in connection with an exciting experimental educational project known as the Midwest Program on Airborne Television Instruction (MPATI). I had been unemployed at the time. My wife and I had prayed earnestly about the job, and we felt quite confident about it, so much so that it was the only job for which I had applied. My wife was a West Lafayette girl, and we wanted to get back into this community. Both of us were blessed with an inner peace that even astonished the two of us. We were gratified for the employment, but not surprised. In retrospect it's amazing, given our spiritual immaturity at the time.

Several years later, when MPATI ceased to be a viable entity, it was necessary to close it down and for me to find other employment. We did not want to leave West Lafayette, and so we prayed that there might be a job opening at Purdue University for which I might be qualified. The odds were not good; times were not flush; the university was hiring very few people. No one was particularly encouraging. We experienced the same calmness and assurance as when we had first signed on. Somehow, it did not surprise us when I was told a position had been created so that I might be hired. And we praised God.

In all of these years, what have I learned? Way too much for expositing in this writing. My experience, of course, is unique, because God deals differently with each one of us. God works in my life in a completely different way than in the lives of any who may chance to read this. Yet I give you three lessons I have learned.

First, I have come to believe that God is sovereign,

capable of doing anything, anytime, anywhere, in any way. God is bigger than our wildest imagination, compounded, to the nth degree!

Second, God is mystery. There is more to God than can ever fully be understood by humankind in all its wisdom and expertise. I am amazed at the things God allows us to do. His Holy Spirit works in our lives in mysterious ways. Our awareness of those workings is, almost without exception, discernible only in retrospect. God is in charge of the so-called coincidences.

Third, be intentional and deliberate in carving out time to be with the Lord. That can take many forms, such as daily Bible study, contemplative silence, a walk in the woods. Develop a routine that provides a regular opportunity to be in communion with the Blessed Trinity. Learning to be present to the presence of God succumbs to no pat formula. There are many techniques. It takes time. And, as a wise retreat leader once commented, it takes time to learn that it takes time. But it is well worth the effort.

Preparing for Death with Legal and Financial Issues
Dallas Oswalt[72]

Transitions and healing are made easier when there has been advance planning about legal and financial matters related to death. For any one person, the pertinent information depends on the legal or other arrangements the person has made independently, with one's spouse, or with professional advisors. Dallas considers the following items most useful and advises starting now to collect the

---

[72] Dallas Oswalt was the vocational agriculture teacher at Wayne Township School and then vice principal at the Teacher Training College. Later, he was assistant field secretary of the mission and principal of Waka Secondary School for the Church of the Brethren in Nigeria. After that he was training program leader at the International Crops Research Institute for the Semi-Arid Tropical near Hyderabad, India. He attended Manchester College and earned a bachelor of science degree at Purdue University. He earned a master's degree and PhD degree from Purdue University. He has two children, three grandchildren, and three great-grandchildren. His wife is deceased and is described later in a poem.

listed information, before a crisis or loss when thinking and memory are blurred.

- Documents with comments, location, telephone or e-mails. Location of originals to be known to survivors.

- Current vita including service, employment, awards, memberships, publications.

- Family history, with grandparents, parents, spouse, children, grandchildren, including birth and death dates, ethnic origin.

- Funeral, cremation, or donation arrangements (funeral home will need to be contacted immediately upon death) with number of death certificates required and ethnic origin; plot identification (showing name, location, and arrangements made).

- Military service records and persons to notify, with description of what to expect.

- General durable power of attorney document, effective upon execution.

- Memorials.

- Durable power of attorney for health care.

- Will (no action if a trust has been made and accounts are held jointly).

- Revocable living trust (recommended to prevent probate).

- Quit claim deed (to be recorded to transfer property into a trust or to individuals).

- Social Security number and benefits information. (Upon a death of a senior, the Social Security Administration should be notified *within* the month of death to stop the next payment due at the end of each month. The last payment should be the one made at the end of previous month. Anyone else entitled to benefits such as a death benefit or continuation of the larger of the payments to spouses should also address the matter with Social Security.)

- Birth certificate (originals are available by phone at health services department of county where born).

- Marriage certificates.

- Prior year's income tax and W-2 forms.

- Life insurance.

- Health insurance.

- Long-term care insurance.

- Property deed.

- Car title or lease.

- Car insurance.

- Driver's license and voter registration.

- Retirement funds.

- Pre-arranged pay on death (POD) arrangement at bank. (This could enable someone to pay bills from your account if you are unable. It is preferred to having a second person on the account, as it avoids involving a second person in liabilities.)

- Broker.

- Churches.

- Schools' alumni offices.

- Newspapers to notify.

Our Sister Jean

I (Flora L. Williams) wrote this poem upon the death of the wife of the writer of the earlier provided estate planning list of Dallas Oswalt.. I read the poem at her funeral.

Our sister in Christ, Jean Oswalt,
We heard, died the other day.
Slipping away to sail with the Divine.
She is nearer to the heart of God
But from us, farther away.
Before Jean saw in a mirror dimly
But now sees God face to face.
What was once a mystery
Now is gloriously relayed.

We can still see sister Jean.
She is not gone forever.
We see in gifts she left behind:

Her strong, brilliant children,
Her lively grandchildren,
Her future great grandchildren.

In memories of Jean
Comforting and inspiring us,
From time to time;
In recordings of her
Determined, kind voice;
In decisions made with
An intelligent mind.

Her soft, assuring words,
Melodic cheery laughter,
Dignity in her actions,
Skills in artistic arrangements.

Her quiet strength
And patient guidance,
Courage to command,
Wisdom shared with mankind.

Bible studies in her home,
Teaching classes and everywhere—
Testimonies to her faith,
Love of God and neighbor.

We thank you, Sister Jean
For gifts enriching all mankind,
For our times together,
As mother, grandmother,
Aunt, sister, wife, and friend,
For your life which shared
Love and many delights!

Sister Jean, you live forever
In our deep love, which
Death can never, ever sever!

Facing Death:
Reflections on the Process
Ruth Anne Friesen[73]

Let us face the reality that death is everywhere. We can be renewed and healed by better verbalizing and understanding the normal event. Below is a dramatic conversation

---

[73] Ruth Anne Friesen wrote this piece November 28, 2012. It is printed here by permission.

Ruth Anne Friesen describes herself as follows: My early home was in Elizabethtown, PA, where I was heartily involved in the Church of the Brethren and graduated from Elizabethtown College. Camp Swatara was a favorite place, too. Peggy and Julius Belser invited me to Reba Place Fellowship, and my involvement here has had significant impact on my life! I married Richard Friesen in 1982 (I married into a Mennonite mission family) and graduated from Bethany Seminary in 1983. We were sent to various mission activities/adventures—the Overground Railroad in south Texas; MCC in San Juan Cotzal, Guatemala; Mennonite Mission Network in the Argentine Chaco. In both Guatemala and Argentina we were working with indigenous people. My husband Richard died August 11, 2010, in Argentina. He was buried in an indigenous cemetery in the village where the three Toba translators with whom he worked originated. Now I am involved *involving a voice of death, a voice of creature, and a voice of narrator.*

Death: I am stalking the land ... hither and yon ... there really is no place I do not cover, from the depths of the oceans to the heights of the mountain peaks ... no one can hide ... my search is ongoing and sometimes surprising ... everyone falls prey!

Creature: Yes, your threat is real! I see you, Death, all around me ... I'm aware of you in many different places, especially here in the hospital. You strike anxiety ... fear ... terror ... in the hearts and lives of many ... both patients and families, doctors and nurses, chaplains and priests, all of us who see you regularly, observe your threats and your actions. What's more we human creatures know well that we all must die one day. We all know that we are only mortal creatures, and each new day brings us closer to our own death. Even Psalm 89, which talks of God's steadfast love and faithfulness, God's covenant, still expresses wonderment about God hiding and whether God's anger and

---

in clinical pastoral education at Rush University Medical Center, Chicago, in May 2013, having completed three units.

wrath burn always. Then it continues on commenting that no one can live forever and never die ... no one can free oneself from the power of death.[1]

Death: Hee ... hee ... heee ... I do seem to strike terror wherever I go. People do seem to want to keep their distance as long as possible. Just as Psalm 55 describes my work, I do often cause hearts to groan in anguish as terror sinks in and fear and trembling take their toll.

Creature: And even Psalm 103, which carries the theme of blessing the Lord for all the Lord's actions on our behalf, still notes that our mortal life is like the grass of the field that flourishes like a flower, but as soon as the wind blows, it ceases to exist. It is gone, never to be seen again.[2] It all seems pretty grim! What a way to live ... fearing death that's going to take its toll no matter what! There's really no escape from death's terror! There really is no way to avoid death! You claim our lives whether we are ready or not to die! There is no choice! We are doomed to the terror and fear of death! It is death that stalks the hallways, elevators, patients' rooms, emergency department ... really every part of the hospital.

Death: At least, all of you mortal creatures are aware of my power and the anxiety and fear that is generated by my stalking through the hospital and through the lives of each one of you!

Creature: Yes, we're aware! But, you know our awareness doesn't stop us from assessing what we observe here at the hospital and in our culture, as well as our responses to this fear ... you might even go so far as to say our slavery to this fear of death.

Narrator: Now, your naming it "slavery to the fear of death" surely makes it sound as though we humans have little choice ... as if we've been sold into this slavery to death and the terrors that surround death.

Creature: That is basically true in our culture, isn't it? We do live in a society where self-protection is important. Our identity, our self-esteem, our possessions all are important to protect. In fact, war is generated when our values seem to be threatened and we are scared. So we pretty immediately try to defend ourselves and our group. We wouldn't want our value systems criticized nor our group members threatened or demonized. So we strive for significance, meaning, and self-esteem.

Narrator: It seems that you're waxing rather theoretical as you talk about how we humans are slaves to the fear of death.

Creature: Perhaps to put it simply: When our belief systems are called into question, anything that makes us anxious brings out our hostility toward others and soon we are trapped, feeling threatened and motivated by fear. This threat and this fear lead to violence, sin, loss, and death.

Narrator: Well, what would our identity look like if we were not trapped by this fear of death? Is it possible to wonder what the human creature would be like if not so entangled by slavery to the fear of death?

Creature: You mean can we imagine what a person would be like who is not hostile toward others nor feeling neither trapped nor fearful about death? Can it be that such a possibility exists in our culture or in our world?

Narrator: I suspect that as humans, there are choices to be made and there is freedom to make choices when people are not so entangled in fear that they are unable to think or to settle into their hearts and listen.

Creature: Now there's a new perspective ... that of choice and freedom! Wonder how we get loose from the slavery and reach to those alternatives?

Narrator: Well, a few minutes ago, I thought I heard you quote from Psalm 103 about the fading flower ceasing its existence. You well know, Ruth Anne, because you memorized it in Spanish, that psalm also talks about the love of the Lord as eternal for those who honor the Lord and the Lord's justice as infinite throughout all the generations![3]

Death: Wait a minute—I don't want you to forget that you saw before in Psalm 103 that the flower quickly fades and dies and that there's no way to avoid death. There's no escape from death's terror!

Creature: True, we humans are merely mortal and we all have to face death. But I think the point that is also made in Psalm 103 is that God's love is eternal, it's a faithful love, and that God's justice does operate down through the generations!

Death: Remember there's still no escape!

Creature: Quiet a minute. You know there are ways to *value life* ... to risk being vulnerable and not being so worried about my self-esteem, but making the choice to be involved in the lives of others ... perhaps even to master anxiety as I open myself to others' needs and values. In fact, probably as I learn more about how to love, perhaps that's when I experience a real loss of self, because I'm not so worried and fearful about myself.

Narrator: Well, that all sounds good, but is it real? Are you serious?

Creature: Seems like I remember that Saint Francis thought it quite possible to make the choice to live simply, giving away possessions, and finding ways to care for others. "O Divine Master, grant that I may not so much seek to be consoled as to console; to be understood as to understand; to be loved as to love. For it is in giving that we receive; it is in pardoning that we are pardoned; and it is in dying that we are born to eternal life."[4]

And it appears that Jesus' life, too, is a solid example of one who risked making choices that were not popular for his time and in his culture. Jesus clearly was enabled to do what he needed to do as he responded to his Father's wishes. In effect, his identity was formed by the Father, and he was not driven by anxieties. Jesus acted out of freedom; he was free to love no matter what the consequences.

Narrator: Yeah, but here you've given examples of a saint and of the Son of God! Really now, how do any of us measure up to those examples?

Creature: Well, is measuring up the qualification or is it more how we make choices and the freedom we have to make choices that value life as a gift?

Narrator: It all sounds very radical! And is the radical even possible?

Creator: You mean for common folks like you and me? Well, let me ask you a further question. Have you noticed that the Gospels are presenting a rather radical perspective? The good news of the Gospels is radical!

And yet, on those very pages of the Gospels we also meet common folks dealing with ordinary day by day issues and meeting the real issues of faith in whatever daily happenings they are facing. In the hospital here, too, we also meet those real people with everyday needs ... like the forty-nine-year-old MS patient who can't move his limbs like he used to and whose pride, he says, still keeps him from asking for help ... like the twenty-six-year-old woman who has stopped drinking but still needs an apartment and a job in order to retrieve three of her children from foster care through a court order ... the eighty-six-year-old priest experiencing *pain* from shingles and from sciatica in his right knee and wondering whether some degree of pain will be his thorn to bear ...

Probably these are the issues of faith that involve the everyday needs of folks we've met and come to know. William Stringfellow comments in his book *Free in Obedience* that "the real issues of faith have to do with the everyday needs of (people) in the world and with the care for and service of those needs ... The real issues of faith have to do with how people are 'harassed by the premonition of death.' The premonition of death takes many forms—from addiction to unemployment to loneliness to marital conflict to paying the bills to disillusionment with the church. Here is where the church should be active."[5]

Narrator: So you're wondering whether we are active in faith. As people work in the hospital environment, you're suspecting that a faith that's put into action is what makes a difference in how we can and do respond to death.

Death: Remember, there's still no escape. I'm always on the prowl and looking for my next victim!

Creature: Well, it's really an upside-down kingdom that makes gain in the Gospels and that gives life to people who were considered outcasts. And it's folks whom you'd least expect to stand tall to the truth of it all who become the witnesses to what they have experienced … they are the enthusiastic ones. It's all rather opposite of what you'd imagine! The cross becomes the sacramental sign of life even in the midst of death and despair. And life is given or gifted as ordinary people learn how to serve and care for others, becoming radically involved in the world as they give their own life away without expecting anything in return.

Narrator: So how are they giving their life away … say more about that. And how does life spring forth from the discouragement and despair of approaching death?

Creature: It has to do with self-giving in *love* … the giving of oneself to be with others in pain without being threatened by the suffering. The willingness to choose to not be concerned with self-interest, but freed to be there for the other person's sake, no matter what is shared from the common events of life. It really is a witness to the possibility of choosing freedom from slavery to the fear of death, because there is a freedom gained in overcoming self-interest and in caring for others! What's really gifted is the grace that flows from God, not from our own efforts. And furthermore, the presence that any of us offer is the gift of Jesus' presence with us always that's promised at the end of the gospel of Matthew.

Narrator: Wow! That's radical stuff! Does it really work … that is, is it possible to put such radical faith to work?

Death: Yeah ... just being radical doesn't mean you will win in the end! Remember everyone faces death. Everyone dies!

Creature: Well, allow me to also comment some from Henri Nouwen's perspective when he wrote to his father six months after his mother's death. As Nouwen writes on Good Friday, he realizes that Jesus had quite a struggle in the garden before his capture as, gripped with fear, he pleaded with God to take this cup away. His agony was intense. Then, on the cross, Jesus cried out, "My God, my God, why have you deserted me?" The clear sense we get is that Jesus did not want to die! Nouwen says, "I came to realize that Christ himself entered with us into the full experience of the absurdity of death ... He never spoke about death as something to be accepted gladly."[6]

Death: Yeah ... Even Jesus died! The agony and fear of death is real ... that's for sure!

Creature: "Although we have to see how death has been part of our life since birth," writes Nouwen, "it remains the greatest unknown in our existence.

Although we have to search for the meaning of death, our protest against it reveals that we will never be able to give it a meaning that can take our fear away."[7]

Death: See! That's just my point. I win! I will continue to stalk the earth and cause fear and misery as long as the earth exists, and that may be a looooong time!

Creature: I need to insist on quiet again! ... ... Now then ... Nouwen goes on to describe his mother's faithful devotion to God through daily communion and prayer times. Then he aptly describes how he imagines God relates to death as he talks about God gifting life! "Death does not belong to God. God did not create death. God does not want death. God does not desire death for us. In God there is no death. God is a God of life. He is the God of the living and not of the dead. Therefore, people who live a deeply spiritual life, a life of real intimacy with God, must feel the pain of death in a particularly acute way. A life with God opens us to all that is alive. It makes us celebrate life; it enables us to see the beauty of all that is created; it makes us desire to always be where life is.

"Death, therefore, must be experienced by a really

religious person neither as a release from the tension of life nor as an occasion for rest and peace, but as an absurd, ungodly, dark nothingness. Now I see why it is false to say that a religious person should find death easy and acceptable. Now I understand why it is wrong to think that a death without struggle and agony is a sign of great faith. These ideas do not make much sense once we realize that faith opens us to the full affirmation of life and gives us an intense desire to live more fully, more vibrantly, and more vigorously."[8]

I well remember how comforting and reassuring this section of Nouwen was as I contemplated God's part in death, and how a God of love could possibly be involved in death. Did God ever bring about or will someone's death? How could that possibly make any sense?

Death: Well ... some of what Nouwen says makes sense and is real ... especially the part about the struggle and agony ... at least that's realistic!

Creature: Yes, for once I agree with you that facing death is a struggle ... but the part that Nouwen is emphasizing is that God is connected to life and gifting life to the full!

Narrator: So how does that gifting happen? In the not yet that we really don't know about and can't yet imagine?

Creature: Well, the irony of the whole story for Christians is, as Nouwen says, "what seemed to be the end proved to be the beginning; what seemed to be a cause for fear proved to be a cause for courage; what seemed to be defeat proved to be victory, and what seemed to be the basis for despair proved to be the basis for hope."[9] And in these statements, Nouwen is talking about the miracle of that Easter morning when the friends of Jesus had their lives completely changed and turned around by Jesus' resurrection from the dead!

So Nouwen goes on to write about the gravity of the change in death because of the resurrection—that love is stronger than death! It is the same love that causes us to mourn and protest as death takes over that later frees us to live in hope. And it is love and hope that give us eyes to see, ears to hear, and spirits to believe as we experience and recognize Presence in our midst. So *life* in the Spirit of the risen Christ is what we give witness to as we are present with others in their mourning and despair. The divine love that dwells in our hearts is what enables us to be present to others. And this great love is stronger than death.

Narrator: That's rather radical again—the possibility of being present to others in love ... a love that's gifted because the Spirit of Jesus is present!

Creature: I remember as I had sessions with the grief counselor there was comment about needing a "container of hope." When all seems to be lost ... and the waves of grief don't quit ... and hope seems destroyed as well ... that's when it's especially important to find a "container of hope," ... someone who can listen without judging ... someone who can be encouraging ... someone who is willing to just be with/be present whether words are spoken or not. I suspect that chaplains and pastors perhaps are the persons who most often become the containers of hope in the hospital setting.

It's often good to know where hope is to be found. The description of being present from Revelation 21 is hopeful! "Then I heard a loud voice call from the throne, 'Look, here God lives among human beings.

He will make his home among them; they will be his people, and he will be their God, God-with-them. He will wipe away all tears from their eyes; there will be no more death, and no more mourning or sadness or pain. The world of the past has gone.'"[10] Clearly it is hard to know what John's vision signifies and what it means. But it certainly draws the attention of those of us who have experienced death close up and have known the mourning and tears. And it surely is encouraging as we continue to face death … sometimes with the faith of the resurrection … and sometimes in doubt … but above all clinging to God's love and presence.

Narrator: But you've just said that faith and doubt are often not so far apart. In fact, they often seem quite connected. That reminds me of Frederick Buechner's comments: "Faith is a way of waiting—never quite knowing, never quite hearing or seeing, because in the darkness we are all but a little lost. There is doubt hard on the heels of every belief, fear hard on the heels of every hope."[11]

Creature: You're right … Buechner's comments do summarize what often seems to happen on the grief journey. One can never be too sure that faith with its assurances of unconditional love and resurrection power will win throughout the day, because challenges often arise that seem to cloud over the light and raise questions. And so there is some battling as doubt arises once again and assails the stronghold.

Death: Good to hear you admit that fear and doubt never are completely wiped out.

Narrator: In those battles, recognizing that the struggle seems fierce and the resistance strong, we might recall Dylan Thomas' spirit: "Do not go gentle into that good night ... Rage, rage against the dying of the light."[12]

Creature: Yet we all wait and trust that we are loved and cared for by One whom we hope to meet as our journey nears home. Even sometimes some minor miracles do show up and offer respite beyond our expectations. For example, after a *lectio divina* session that focused on Jesus walking on the water, I was aware that every morning as I ride a bicycle up to Northwestern University, I sometimes am out on the stretch by the lake and head right toward the lake and onto the lake. That's when I ride on water! My heart and spirit are certainly out there on the water as I yell, "Yes, Lord. Yes!" And that's a Yes to whatever the call may be in that day.

Narrator: So it's your experience that there is a gracious Presence that accompanies you.

Creature: Sure! There's a Jim Croegaert song that affirms that "The Lord Is with Us":

> Hidden from sight, we affirm and believe
> The Lord is with us
> The Lord is with us
> Bearing us through every loss we may grieve
> The Lord is with us
> The Lord is with us
> With might to protect us
> With strength to defend us
> The Lord is with us … …[13]

So, then, as I learn to be present to each moment and to cherish each moment, I find sparkles of life appearing in common and even unlikely places. It is often those sparkles that ignite new hope and help me to rejoice in my being accompanied by a gracious Presence that has promised never to abandon me. Perhaps I am enabled then more and more to rest in the assurance that I am the Lord's whether I live or whether I die. Both in Romans 14:7–9 and in 1 Thessalonians 5:10 I hear that "in life and in death we belong to the Lord."[14] I may still experience fear as I face death, but there certainly are reassurances of faith and resurrection that bring hope. And music and songs recall the hope, as well!

Narrator: There's another piece of music that expresses hope rather profoundly. Natalie Sleeth wrote "In the Bulb There Is a Flower":[15]

> In the bulb there is a flower, in the seed, an apple tree;
> In cocoons, a hidden promise: butterflies will soon be free!
> In the cold and snow of winter there's a spring that waits to be,
> Unrevealed until its season, something God alone can see.

> There's a song in ev'ry silence, seeking word and melody.
> There's a dawn in ev'ry darkness, bringing hope to you and me.
> From the past will come the future; what it holds a mystery.
> Unrevealed until its season, something God alone can see.
>
> In our end is our beginning; in our time, infinity;
> In our doubt there is believing; in our life, eternity.
> In our death, a resurrection; at the last, a victory,
> Unrevealed until its season, something God alone can see.

What a profound way to envision the thinness that exists between time and eternity and the mystery that life to the full really holds in the now and in the not yet!

---

[1] Psalm 89:46–49. Dios Habla Hoy: La Biblia Versión Popular. *God Speaks Today: The Popular Bible Version.* Nueva York: Sociedad Biblica Americana. 1979, p. 719.

[2] Psalm 103:15–16. Ibid. p.728.

[3] Psalm 103:17. Ibid.

[4] Prayer of St. Francis of Assisi. "Lord Make Me an Instrument of Your Peace … …"

5. From blog of Richard Beck, "Experimental Theology," *The William Stringfellow Project: Free in Obedience*, Part 1.
6. Nouwen, Henri J. M. *A Letter of Consolation*. New York, NY: Harper & Row, Publishers, Inc. 1982. p. 71–72.
7. Ibid. p. 73.
8. Ibid. p. 75–76.
9. Ibid. p. 91.
10. Revelations 21:3–4. *The New Jerusalem Bible: Standard Edition*. New York: Doubleday, 1998, p. 1404.
11. Buechner, Frederick on August 1. Hickman, Martha. *Healing after Loss*. New York: HarperCollins Publishers. 1994.
12. Thomas, Dylan from *The Poems of Dylan Thomas*. Cambridge, MA: New Directions Publishing Co., 1952 in *Patches of Godlight*.
13. Croegaert, Jim and Adam, David. "The Lord Is with Us." © 1997, Rough Stones Music.
14. Romans 14:7–9 and 1 Thessalonians 5:10. *Dios Habla Hoy*. p. 233 and 297.
15. Sleeth, Natalie, "In the Bulb There Is a Flower," *Hymnal: A Worship Book*. Brethren Press. © 1986 Hope Publishing Co., Carol Stream, IL 60188. All rights reserved. Used by permission.

Bibliography

There is a lot of life experience and reading that goes into this paper. It really is impossible to capture all of the readings and reflections, but here is a try at some of them:

Doka, Kenneth J. and Davidson, Joyce D. (Eds.) *Living with Grief: Who We Are, How We Grieve.* Philadelphia, PA: Brunner/Mazel. 1998 Hospice Foundation of America.

Hickman, Martha Whitmore. *Healing after Loss: Daily Meditations for Working through Grief.* New York: HarperCollins Publishers Inc., 1994. Buechner, Frederick quote—August 1.

Johnson, Rayborn (conducting the interview) with Beck, Richard. *Beyond the Box.* Podcast.com. Three part series *The Slavery of Death*: 1) The Sting of Death Is

Sin—May 28, 2012, 2) The Denial of Death—June 3, 2012, 3) Perfect Love Casts Out Fear—June 13, 2012.

Messer, Donald E. "Patches of Godlight." *Reflections on Grief and Spiritual Growth*. Edited by Weaver, Andrew J. and Stone, Howard W. Nashville: Abingdon Press, 2005. p. 79–87.

Nouwen, Henri J. M. *A Letter of Consolation*. New York, NY: Harper & Row, Publishers, Inc. 1982.

Prayer of Saint Francis of Assisi. "Lord make me an instrument of your peace …"

Slough, Rebecca, Mgr. Ed. *Hymnal: A Worship Book*. Brethren Press, Elgin, IL. Newton, KS: Faith and Life Press, Scottsdale, PA: Mennonite Publishing House. 1992. "In the Bulb There Is a Flower," p. 614.

Spiro, Howard M., McCrea Curnen, Mary G., and Palmer Wandel, Lee (Eds.). *Facing Death: Where Culture, Religion, and Medicine Meet*. Boston, MA: Yale University, 1996.

Stringfellow, William, *Free in Obedience* from blog Beck, Richard, "Experimental Theology."

"The Lord Is with Us." Music by Croegaert, Jim and words by Adam, David. Refrain from THE OPEN GATE, Celtic Prayers for Growing Spiritually by David Adam and Croegaert, Jim. © 1997, Rough Stones Music.

Caregiving Challenge and Charm
Marie Willoughby

My husband and I are not hindered by embarrassment and reluctance. We just have to ask for help when we need it. And there are some days when help isn't needed.

For us, this more intimate caring for bodily needs began when my husband fell and broke both arms. Of course, the nurses and aides in the hospital and care center tended to bodily functions initially. He was seventy-five years old, and I was seventy-four. We'd been married for almost fifty-two years by then. But, as most independent adults do, we took care of our bodily needs ourselves before this.

There are many things that limit one's ability as the person ages. Falling is just one of the hazards of getting older. And it does happen, more than we want to admit. Besides the disappointments of not able to follow through on your plans for vacations and commitments, the results of falls put strains on the rest of the body, and on your relationship with those around you. Depression, frustration, pain, energy level—all change. All ebb and flow unpredictably. You yell, you complain, you apologize, you mope. Sometimes you even throw things, then feel very badly about having done it. You just can't do everything you want to do. And you do things you don't want to do. Both of you. But love never ends. And now is a time for it to grow. It grows in ways you never expected.

For weeks, my husband had to have someone else feed him, which one can tolerate when both arms are in slings, However, on a continuing basis, my husband also needs assistance with bathing and toileting. These are not nearly as easy to manage—both in the giving and the receiving. As healing occurs, not everything comes back as it was before. Limitations continue in many cases. So the need never goes away. Bathing can be worked out. Getting at all the private places can be learned and accepted. It can even be a joy to help each other manage this. Washing, drying, applying lotions, putting on support stockings—whatever makes for comfort and relief. But the toileting can be a problem. Holding a urinal so it works right. Wiping a bottom isn't fun for anyone, even doing it for yourself. The need is there, so we just accept it and get on with it. We've done this for our infants; now we do it for our spouse. To be "willing and ready" to help when the need occurs, without anger, rancor, or regret, is so important. These things take only a few minutes of our time. Doing them willingly, and lovingly, and not making any kind of fuss about all of it, can make our older life together sweet. Tender loving care is always important, but especially now as we care for one another.

What do I as a caregiver get in return? A nice back rub or a foot massage. Many words of appreciation. A relaxed and nonresistant patient. The one receiving these ministrations helps the caregiver so much by having an accepting attitude. After all, what else can we do but what needs to be done? Someday it will be my turn to need this kind of intimate help. Remembering, accepting, loving, aging. You can decide how you face this. Be kind.

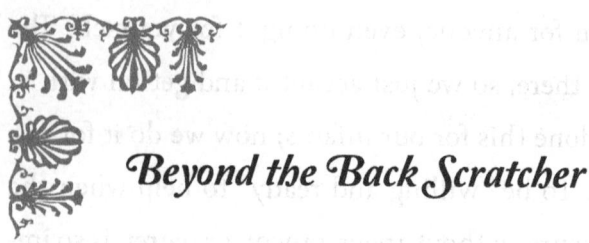

Beyond the Back Scratcher

Renewal is assisted when we make physical arrangements with helpful tools. In the Scriptures, 2 Corinthians 4:16–18 proclaims renewal and power by elevating the spiritual arena over the physical. Those verses point out that Christians inwardly "are being renewed day by day." In addition to spiritual influences, there are mental powers each of us have, which can override the material and the physical arenas.

One way to have mind prevail over the physical or bodily conditions is to replace attitudes. For example, if you have the habit of thinking "I can't," change to "I think I can; I think I can." Philippians 4:13 says, "I can do all this through Him who gives me strength."

Another way to exercise the mental over the physical conditions is to choose mechanical and electronic instruments or other implements to provide strength and power. These include the following:

- Back scratcher to reach and comfort
- Medical alert pendant to call for help if you fall or are threatened
- Blinds in windows at your home—if you pull up the blinds each day, unopened blinds can signal the mail carrier or others that you may be incapacitated inside
- Grabber or reacher tools
- Canes; wheelchairs; motorized scooters
- Step stools or walkers to help you get up
- Cell phone; cameras for others to check on your movements and conditions
- Doorbell that has two-way intercom speaker
- BiPAP or CPAP breathing device
- Hospital bed or mattress that prevents bed sores
- Shoes with Velcro fasteners
- Rugs that prevent slipping or tripping
- Grab bars; ramps
- Pill dispenser boxes
- Voice translator; hearing aids
- Magnifying glass for reading labels; reading projector with variable magnifier

If we grow older without also growing wiser, our hearts may become hardened. We can become blinded to the signs and wonders of God, skeptical of intervention, less alert to see where God's hand is moving. We may increasingly think we cannot do something because of our health and other problems. We may lose our confidence or think we are inadequate. We fail to see the *delights* God has given, because we are stuck on ourselves and our problems.

Another suggestion is to change or redesign the work and other activities so as to simplify, be efficient, and reduce effort; this can free the spirit for more important endeavors (idea by Ellen Richards, an early founder of home economics). The core principle of work simplification is to work smarter, not harder. There is always a better way. Be God-abled, not disabled. "I can do all things through Christ who strengthens me." This implies doing things differently than in a previous time.

The first of the mental tools to change work/life activities is to eliminate certain activities or change standards, such as long hair to short. The second is to rearrange storage or placement for ease and safety. The third is to combine activities or trips. The fourth is to simplify actions, arrangements, storage, meals, and so on. Think about how basic tasks of work or other activities can be made yet simpler. For example, you might design a simpler way to comb or brush your hair. Renewal of mind and spirit is accomplished by new systems and procedures.

Challenging experiences and frustrations lead to understanding and suggestions for others. Of course, the greatest resources are the mind, creativity, and hope, which bring energy.

In pep talks to myself, I say, "I can do it—not like before—but I can do it," through tears and sweat. The difficult journey is new, slow, frustrating, and tiring—like learning a foreign language. By repeating motions, the new method becomes automatic. As I age, the most important cane to lean on is my determination. The pull of the journey onward depends upon renewed vigor to do normal tasks differently.

The road signs along the way read "Work Smarter, Not Harder," "There Is Always a Better Way," "Use Your Brain, Not Your Body," and "Convenience, Not Convention." Such slogans were drilled into my head when I taught a university course for restaurant/hotel managers and for those working with the disabled.

Students would observe the original method and then with charts and tools develop improved methods for hand and body motions. The objective was improvement by eliminating unnecessary motions, combining motions, rearranging supplies, and simplifying. When I taught my classes, I dealt with theory, but practice for me is now a necessity.

The challenge is not only to accomplish a task but also to shorten time, decrease stress, or improve productivity. Meeting that challenge is sometimes tearful and tiring. As I have no right hand, I am often exhausted from using my left hand and arm continuously. Often, too tired after showering and dressing, I have to rest before continuing. Simple screwing on of a lid and other little tasks are not so simple, because my brain and hand motions are reversed or mixed up and I lack the support of the other hand. The complexities of operating in a different world are experienced by all who try with only one awkward hand and an already programmed brain. The determined say, "I can do everything I did before—it just takes longer."

The journey can be approached with humor rather than fear. Putting on a bra using one hand was no easy task, but I changed the method by hooking it first and placing it over my head. One day, however, I got trapped in it, not able to pull it down with my left hand. I panicked and rushed downstairs, yelling to my husband for help. But by then, the bra had worked itself down during the commotion.

The better method for getting dressed is to ask my husband to help me, as by pulling up my support hose for me and assisting with various clothing fasteners. That starts the day with a delightful togetherness journey.

Nevertheless, I have had to develop skills for *living independently* rather than remaining in frustration.

When my children were little, I taught them the song that cautions: "Stop, look, and listen before you cross the street." Now I sing, "Ponder in prayer, not panic, prior to proceeding."

Examples of changing are numerous. Day by day, I ponder what no longer has to be folded, what different materials make for more ease, and what is adequate if not necessarily ideal. My family is surprised at new storage arrangements such as laying clothes on a suitcase in the dressing room rather than folding them neatly for drawers. The ends of bread wrappers are merely folded now, not secured by manipulating a twist tie. Every move is calculated. I even use my head to apply pressure to a door when turning the key.

Working in the kitchen required many adjustments. My teeth became vital equipment for tearing open packages. Biting off the ends of green beans rather than cutting them was faster. Closing drawers or doors with a knee rather than a hand represented the principle of *combining*. Potatoes stay in the sink and I push the brush against them, using my thumb to pick out bad spots. I don't peel potato skins; they stay on for the mashing, which is the style now at my home. Smaller pitchers are prettier and easier for my overused arm to carry. When I remember, I use my stub to carry, lift, or brace against something.

Performing at my desk forced innovation. To open an envelope, I now use my hand to place one end of the envelope between my teeth, then I pick up the letter opener and slice. For various tasks, I make one hand serve as two, using my thumb and index finger to grasp or move one thing while using the last three fingers on something else. Headphones became indispensable for taking notes.

Analyzing the desktop arrangement and the process was critical for reading a book and taking notes.

First, I couldn't keep a book open (and I am still seeking the best angle to position books and papers). A friend gave me a simple tool for holding pages open. Also, having the right chair with the correct height is a must for writing and for my back's endurance.

My car, with all the controls on the left side of the dashboard or on the steering wheel, made driving hundreds of miles per week possible. My stub could apply enough pressure to turn a handle or even guide the steering wheel for a short time. My teeth would hold the seat belt shoulder strap until I clicked the belt latch into place.

Getting ready for the day demanded creative thought, even when I was still half asleep. To dry my back after bathing, I can hold a small towel by end and slap my back with it. I don't move a fingernail file or nail brush back and forth on a fingernail; instead I move my finger back and forth over the implement, held in place against a flat surface with my stub. Ironing was out; stretch fabrics were in. Sometimes I carry a paper cup in my teeth when I need my hand to open the door. I have also learned to carry things squeezed between my stubbed arm and body.

To add ease without sacrificing beauty, I replaced

a heavy comforter on the bed with a lightweight quilt. It's easier now to flip it into place.

At laundry time, I drop the full clothes basket over the railing rather than carrying it downstairs. Then I attach a hanger to drag it to the laundry room.

My stub is becoming a friend as I learn to use it more and more. It is a good place to hang my purse or briefcase temporarily, freeing my left hand for opening doors. When planting in my garden, a new plant stays nestled against my stub while I dig and spread soil using a trowel with my left hand.

The path through the day is easier when it is uncluttered. Barriers are removed. Translated to practicality, this means eliminating things not used, storing infrequently used items in a remote place, and using prime space for prime use. Weekends give opportunity to rearrange furniture, work layouts, and storage for everyday ease.

Eliminating cumbersome long hair in favor of a short cut was another practical change. And jar lids don't have to be screwed on so tightly. Windows need not be closed so tightly.

Family members also had to be trained for these changes. We all had to adjust to new ways for new days.

Eliminating complexity or activities for simpler living helps determine priorities. My overused left hand and arm demand I either give them a rest or use my feet, brain, some tool, or someone to share the work. Solutions for this dilemma, as applied to time, effort, and money, can be summed up in the following options: increase resources; decrease wants; be more efficient; *or continue to be frustrated.* We soon learn we must do it differently, ditch it, or delegate it.

The mandate from Scripture to arrange things for convenience, handicapped accessibility, and "springing forth" is Hebrews 12:12–13 (NKJV): "Therefore strengthen the hands which hang down, and the feeble knees, and make straight paths for your feet, so that what is lame may not be *dislocated,* but rather is healed."

Different translations provide insights and emphases about this everyday issue. The Common English Bible translation presents Hebrews 12:12–13 another way, as follows: "So strength your drooping hands and weak knees! Make straight paths for your feet so that if any part is lame, it will be healed rather than injured more seriously."

The New Living Translation presents the same

passage differently: "So take a new grip with your tired hands and strengthen your weak knees. Mark out a straight path for your feet so that those who are weak and lame will not fall but become strong."

The Good News Translation says, "Lift up your tired hands, then, and strengthen your trembling knees! Keep walking on straight paths, so that the lame foot may not be disabled, but instead be healed."

And *The Message* says, "So don't sit around on your hands! No more dragging your feet! Clear the path for long-distance runners so no one will trip and fall, so no one will step in a hole and sprain an ankle. Help each other out. And run for it."

Hence, we are not "disabled" but are *differently abled.* We are enabled by God and spiritually propelled.

Arise from Addictions

Probably everyone has some type of addiction since everyone has some type of imperfection, brokenness, or incomplete surrender to God. "Addiction is a misdirected spiritual search."[74] Some have addictions of collecting things or doing things that require outlandish sums of money. Things and substances are expensive substitutes for the real thing. Addictions can be of different types. Examples include giving to grandchildren, doing crossword puzzles, and shopping, if they are not meeting real needs and prevent real needs from being met. They may cost one's family, career, savings, financial stability, and life. They could even cost one's soul. Dependency on some addictions affects the chemistry of the body, one's ability to think clearly, habits, and relationships.

A misdirected search for wholeness, meaning in

---

[74] Oliver J. Morgan and Merle Jordan, *Addiction and Spirituality* (St. Louis: Chalice Press, 1999), 66.

life, joy, or relief from pain may result in gambling or other addictions. There might be compulsive behavior and obsession with possessions. All of these are an attempt to fill an emptiness, the void that only Christ and His redeeming love can fill. Compulsion to spend or gamble does not assure more love, better self-esteem, healing of hurts and regrets, or reducing stress in daily living. The compulsion is a search for comfort, power, or winning, or it is an attempt to overcome loneliness, shame and anger. It can be a result of disappointments or being fearful. Obsessive-compulsive disorder is characterized by not distinguishing the important from the unimportant.

Addicted individuals come from all walks of life. A college student came to his pastor begging for help. The student could not stop buying drinks, even though it was making his parents suffer emotionally and financially. Another man, "Bruce," cannot stop for gas without buying lottery tickets (names in these examples have been changed). Mary is trapped by gambling's hold and uses both hands to play two slot machines at once.

Spending, buying, and accumulating bring cascading problems for addicted people and their families.

Jim, a hard-working factory man, periodically has to extract his wife from the mall since she cannot stop buying. Then they have to return things. Amy, a religious individual who regularly reads Scripture and goes to support groups, keeps buying clothes she does not wear and cannot find among her cluttered things. She has not recovered from devastating politics on the job, a low self-concept, obesity, and depression. She suffers from post-traumatic stress disorder. Her professional husband's salary doesn't suffice, as they have thirty-two thousand dollars of credit card debt. Oscar, a professed conservative Christian, asked his parents to pay off his debts from travel so he could get a job. Then he continued to buy and buy for his hobbies and travel. He had expensive tastes in furniture. Now the debt is higher than ever. His job is uncertain. Beatrice, who directs a shelter for battered women and helps them daily, finds her own therapy and relief from continually buying all types of clothes, food, and things for herself. Sue, intending to reassure her grandchildren of her love, buys gifts for them with money she does not have.

Gambling addictions, mentioned earlier, can cause problems in all strata of society. The National

Endowment for Financial Education reports, "On any given night across the country at Gamblers Anonymous meetings sit doctors, lawyers, business owners, executives, and bank presidents."[75] Older Americans who have money and time are showing an increase in gambling to reduce loneliness and boredom.[76]

Money used for gambling may come from pensions and social security for the elderly who later cannot recover financially. Even so, they gamble to escape loneliness, loss of a spouse or other loved one, or a frustrating illness. Many of the poor become hooked in the desperate attempt to gain money. And those in the middle class (oftentimes the men) gamble to repay huge losses.[77] Some people squander life savings, equity in their houses, or use others' money to

---

[75] National Endowment for Financial Education, "Helping the Problem Gambling Client," Supplement to the September 2000 issue of *Journal of Financial Planning*.

[76] Ibid.

[77] The author acknowledges the work of gambling addiction health care professionals Brenda Teasell and Bruce Ballon. Various published observations of theirs are included in this chapter. Teasell and Ballon have been affiliated with the Centre for Addiction and Mental Health, Problem Gambling Project; 416-535-8501 ext. 4550 (Toronto, Ontario, CA).

repay with winnings. Suicides sometimes result when they cannot pay debts. Some gamblers turn to crime such as robbing a bank for their desperate addiction of gambling. Others use pawn shops and pawn family heirlooms.

The *addictive-thought system* holds on to past deprivations, grievances, and worry about the future—having enough money or being liked. The culture, the media, and society convince people they are short on something, lack something, are never enough, or are incomplete. This system tells people they need more money, nicer possessions, a better car, expensive clothes, and external excitement in buying, gambling, and expensive recreation. Advertising and television confirm these feelings and offer endless pursuits to relieve tension, fill emptiness, and provide pleasure.[78] The media is a reflection of "our own collective state of mind." People are under the illusion that something external—outside of us—brings freedom, power, and love.[79] They think happiness is found in obtaining the excitement, substance, possession, or person. Actually the result is fear, as the compulsive "search for happi-

---

[78] Ibid., 196–223.

[79] Morgan and Jordan, *Addiction and Spirituality*, 65–66.

ness in people, things, and substances results in the vicious cycle of fear."[80] Fear is in not being good enough and being rejected, or not being accepted. When this fear is confirmed in words and reactions of family, friends, students, and work associates, ways to distract from the pain are sought. Lack of love, respect, and status among peers, as well as a lack of self-love, drive people to seek escape or lead to deviant behavior.

Substance and process addictions are those intakes and activities that demand more and more to satisfy an individual's cravings, longings, and emotional highs. They are uncontrollable in that an individual cannot stop them even though they are damaging to family relations, family finances, work behavior, job security, and medical health. The addict is one who is consistently unable to make the changes in behavior despite negative consequences. The addiction takes precedence over other values and activities. The person is compelled to follow through on the desires and passions of addictions as though a driving force moves him or her toward the addiction rather than healthier choices. People who are addicted are under the illusion

---

[80] Ibid., 68.

that something external will bring them freedom from pain, healing from past hurts, release from trouble, removal of bad memories, and escape from fear. Some victims are addicted to needing other people's approval in order to feel good about themselves. They have habitual ways to seek approval and so experience great stress when rejected or feeling bad about themselves.[81] Others are simply out of control in several areas of their life.

Addicts have a change in body chemistry, which makes recovery very difficult. There is a chemical change in the brain that reduces the control mechanism. May defines true addictions as "compulsive behaviors that eclipse our concern for God and compromise our freedom, characterized by 'intolerance,' withdrawal symptoms, loss of willpower, and distortion of attention."[82] Other characteristics are self-deception, loss of ability to feel pleasure, hopelessness, denial, repression, rationalization, distortion, a mind that plays tricks, delaying tactics, hiding, crippling

---

[81] Ibid., 37.

[82] Gerald G. May, *Love and Spirituality in the Healing of Addictions* (HarperSanFrancisco, 1988), 37.

behavior, and collusion. In summary, addiction is a disease of the body, mind, and soul.

An addict is one who "is consistently unable to make changes in ... behavior despite increasingly negative consequences in all or some areas of life: medical, legal, relational, economic, vocational, emotional, and spiritual."[83] This situation is considered sin; the person is "disconnected from God, self, and others in a profoundly emotional way."[84]

The addict attempts to meet the longings, the *thirst*, the desire to be loved, respected, and accepted—by accumulating more and more, by uncontrolled spending and buying, or by resorting to various other activities or substances. Frustration and discontent eventually result when the person's deepest longings are unmet in worldly solutions, which are not sourced from the Living Water (Psalm 1).

Some people do not believe Jesus when He says, "Everyone who drinks this water will be thirsty again, but whoever drinks the water I give him will never thirst. Indeed the water I give him will become in

---

[83] Morgan and Jordan, *Addiction and Spirituality*, 66.
[84] Ibid., 196.

him a spring of water welling up to eternal life" (John 4:13–14).

Recovery involves learning to love God more than all else. We do not receive some of the good things that God is giving us, because our hands are too full of addictions to receive them. Addictions fill up our hearts and minds, which otherwise would be filled with grace. They divert our attention and sap our strength.[85] Grace is "the dynamic outpouring of God's loving nature that flows into and through creation in an endless self-offering of healing, love, illumination, and reconciliation. It is a gift that we are free to ignore, reject, ask for, or simply accept."[86] "Grace is ready to transform and empower us even in ordinary situations. Miracles are nothing other than God's ordinary truth seen with surprised eyes."[87] The Spirit changes the desire. The hand of God intervenes in recovery. One of the fruits of the Spirit is self-control.

A simple solution to ending addiction is to just *quit* it, not engaging in the next addictive behavior, and not

---

[85] Ibid., 17.

[86] Ibid.

[87] Ibid., 155.

indulging in the next temptation.[88] One explanation for recovery is: "It is simultaneously the expression of Christ-with-and Spirit-in us, sharing our suffering and restlessness, creating and empowering and living in and through the very cells that make us, preserving our freedom with intimate love in everything we do and are."[89] Recovery takes hard work and a process described below.

To raise awareness of compulsive gambling as a mental health problem, wristbands are being sold to raise money for health-related charities by employees in member casinos nationwide. The National Council on Problem Gambling offers referrals in all fifty states. (Call 1-800-522-4700.) They characterize problem gambling as "a need to bet more money more frequently restlessness or irritability when attempting to stop." Also, they say, "Behavior continues in spite of mounting, serious, and negative consequences."

God, the Great Physician, is seeking to restore wholeness and health. A counselor assists by redirecting addictive behavior, problem gambling, pathological gambling, and compulsive acts by controlling—not always curing.

---

[88] Ibid., 177.
[89] Ibid., 180.

Recovery involves seeking new options, replacing the addiction with new longings. The entire family needs to be involved. Others have been co-addicts in various ways. They have faulty thinking in both culture and basic beliefs, which have to be changed.[90] Denial must cease. Secrets have to be exposed. Energy must be spent on changing rather than fighting. Personal management must be assumed. Respect and dignity usually need to be increased. Control of some addictions, rather than total cure, is possible as long periods of abstinence are possible.[91]

For success, experts recommend a combination of treatments and supportive services, including many of the following:

- intensive individual therapy as well as long-term counseling
- medication for a long term, based on psychiatric evaluation

---

[90] Patrick Carnes, *Out of the Shadows* (Center City, MN: Hazelden, 2001).

[91] Liz Meszaros, "Impulse Control Disorders," in *Gale Encyclopedia of Medicine* (Gale Group, December 2002).

- group therapy self-help programs such as twelve-step and other support groups
- educational classes
- couple therapy
- family therapy
- psychiatric evaluation
- Gamblers Anonymous; Debtors Anonymous
- financial counseling; credit counseling; financial planning services

One of the "first steps in dealing with an addiction is to find the motivation to change." Understanding the emotional trigger that creates the addiction is useful. "Addicts are harboring pent-up emotions, especially anger, and addictive behavior which feels like a release for that anger."[92]

As mentioned above, usually recovery from addiction requires accessing multiple types of treatment or support. In regard to support group programs, the twelve-step program used by Alcoholics Anonymous has proven most successful in the recovery process. The following is a summary of a fifteen-step plan

---

[92] CONCERN (Baptist Memorial Health Care Corporation, 2005).

(adapted from the twelve steps), which applies to any type of addiction:

1. Admitting addictions and desires are unmanageable, pain and buried conflicts are unresolved; overcoming denial.

2. Believing in God or a higher power to restore management and control.

3. Turning over will and life to the care of God in total surrender.

4. Honestly searching the thinking, feeling, shame, guilt, wrongs, poisons, dominating fears, and worldly gods.

5. Admitting and confessing these wrongs and fears to God and to another individual in detail, telling one's story.

6. Preparing the soil of the soul for God to overcome temptations, the negative influence of

others, addictions, bad habits, poor management, wrongs.

7. Humbly asking God to remove these wrongs, obstacles, and fears.

8. Writing a list of people who the addict has harmed, or who have harmed the addict, in preparing the heart to restore communication and remove negative feelings.

9. Making amends to others wherever possible except when it would cause more harm or injury.

10. Admitting and asking forgiveness whenever one continues doing wrong or does not trust God to care.

11. Seeking through prayer and meditation to be sustained by God's love, to follow His will, to resist temptation, to fill the inner emptiness, and be empowered by the Spirit to continue rather than empowered by destructive means.

12. Carrying the message to others and practicing the principles God commanded: not coveting, not being greedy, not having gods of the world. It is being honest, satisfied with God's love, and loving one's neighbor by sharing.

13. Affirming and enjoying one's strengths, talents, and creativity; not hiding these from oneself and others;[93] giving thanks for everything; and recounting the things the person did right during each day with the Spirit's power and the love of Jesus Christ—giving thanks for progress.

14. Accepting that life is not easy and there are ups and downs on the path which are lessons for growth,[94] while the Lord is with us each step of the way.

15. Taking steps to (a) heal finances; (b) organize one's life; (c) avoid situations or people who are hurtful, harmful, or demeaning; (d) have

---

[93] Morgan and Jordan, *Addiction and Spirituality*, 131.
[94] Ibid., 133.

control under God's control; (e) have commitment to change and (f) have joy and peace from Jesus Christ who saves.[95]

People can continue to pray "Keep us from temptation" and from "the evil," which may be the programming, the lure, and the advertisements that would lead them in devastating directions. The Bible, in 1 Timothy 6:9–10, says, "People who want to get rich fall into temptation and a snare, and into many foolish and harmful desires that plunge them into ruin and destruction. For the love of money is a root of all kinds of evil. Some people, eager for money, have wandered from the faith and pierced themselves with much grief."

To address compulsive spending behavior, the *why* has to be sorted out as well as *what* the expenses are and *when* they occurred. Then determine how basic needs can be met in less expensive, more constructive, and more fulfilling ways. Basic needs, those that drove the individual to misdirect the search, include social, psychological, material, health, and spiritual needs.

To treat obsessive-compulsive behavior or that

---

[95] May, *Love and Spirituality in the Healing of Addictions*, 39.

type of disorder, medication and cognitive-behavioral therapy are used. The hypotheses are that the orbital cortex, located at the underside of the brain's frontal lobe, is overactive for those with OCD.[96] An increase in serotonin is needed, so serotonin reuptake inhibitors are used to inhibit the uptake of serotonin back into the pre-synaptic neuron, by clogging the passages. Thus an increased amount of serotonin is in the synaptic cleft between the neurons, and every once in a while, serotonin will be absorbed by the post-synaptic neuron.[97]

Cognitive-behavioral therapy builds the individual's faith in one's own rationalization skills; that is, one's reasoning ability and instinctive responses to certain events. The goals are to reduce fear, refrain from rituals of "acting out," and reduce catastrophic and exaggerated thinking. The therapy attempts to "reduce excessive emotional reactions and self-defeating behavior by modifying the faulty or erroneous thinking and maladaptive beliefs."[98]

---

[96] Joseph Xiong, "Obsessive-Compulsive Behavior and the Types of Treatments," *Serendipity*, January 7, 2002.

[97] Ibid.

[98] This description is from the work of Brenda Teasell and Bruce Ballon; see earlier note.

Progress can be measured by whether the person can handle frustrations and maintain self-control in a given period without engaging in addictions, including addictions of sex, smoking, drinking, eating, gift giving, or other addictions. This self-control is achieved by using alternative methods to obtain self-esteem and worth.

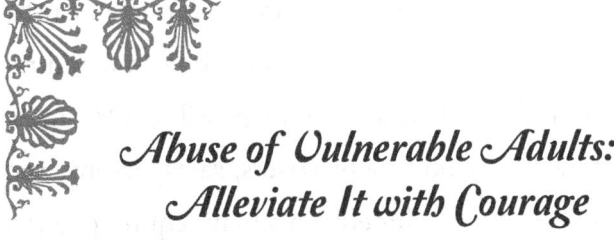

Abuse of Vulnerable Adults: Alleviate It with Courage

We *spring forth* when we heal our emotional hurts, including any afflictions from being abused and exploited. Abuses include being controlled by others, hurt physically, hurt emotionally, hurt financially, or violated personally or legally. We are renewed when we assist others to alleviate their suffering by combating and stopping abuses. We can feel the strength and courage from our Creator in attempting to conquer abuse and in taking action.

Abuse of self in early years increases the chance of being abused in later years. Self-abuse includes neglect of physical care and health needs, not taking necessary medicine, lack of exercise, destructive patterns that may have been learned from parents, and insufficient knowledge. Many victimized people also have insufficient variety of income, insufficient determination to change, and inexperience in taking charge.

Preventive actions include maintaining a healthy lifestyle, remaining mobile the best one can, and remaining independent as long as possible. One must learn how to say no to advertisers, salespersons, and children, even when lonely. This may require practicing by role playing with help of a professional or friend

Becoming *money smart* is following Jesus' teachings to be shrewd. (See 2 Samuel 22:27; Psalm 18:26; Matthew 10:16; Luke 16:18.) This includes knowing what the power of attorney can and cannot do. "If you don't appoint a POA before your decision-making ability declines, a family member or friend might have to go to court to have a guardian appointed. That process can be lengthy, expensive, and very public."[99]

The abusers and exploiters are greedy people—selfish, mean, and unscrupulous. Jesus told us to be "shrewd" as He was sending us out among the wolves. The world is wild and dangerous. Therefore, we need to be educated and daily pray to "not lead us into temptation" and "keep us from the evil one" as taught by Jesus in the Lord's Prayer (Matthew 6:9-13). When we are

---

[99] FDIC (Federal Deposit Insurance Corporation), *Money Smart for Older Adults* (2013), 8.

victimized, we should pray for the next steps to take. We also need to pray for courage.

Abuse is happening to those around us who need rescuing. Abuse happens in every socioeconomic level and occupation. Many people are abused by others and by circumstances outside their control. They are victimized. The forms of abuse, particularly for the elderly, are physical, psychological, emotional, sexual, financial, and depriving older persons of their benefits, belongings, or assets. Common examples of elder abuse include verbal mistreatment, physical neglect, abandonment, refusal of family or church members to visit or to help, not cleaning for the person, withholding medicine, stealing money and valuable possessions, and locking the person in a room.

Self-confidence and ability to do simple tasks decrease with abuse of any type. In social or public situations, the abused might be disrespected by family members or caregivers who interrupt, answer questions directed to the person, and talk for the person. In private, the abused may miss the satisfaction of self-direction and accomplishment when the caregiver insists on doing simple tasks for the person such as simple preparation of food, handling the mail, watering plants, and some activities of dressing.

An abused person gives in to wishes of children or caregivers because the person needs them and is afraid of losing their love. The elderly may be afraid to say *no* to their children or caregivers because the elderly have been physically or emotionally beaten in the past. Some are hit when they wet the bed, say no, or "talk back."

Many put up with abuse because they do not want to get a family member, caregiver, or church in trouble. The abused one is fearful and so is less likely to report a relative who is providing food, giving medicine, and paying rent. The typical case victim is a seventy-year-old woman with an alcoholic son who does not work and is on disability. According to a prosecutor, women will "turn in" a daughter before reporting a son. People who are abused typically have no money with which to move to a safer place, no assets for a nursing home, and an inability to provide for themselves in matters such as getting groceries and using the bathroom.

An abuser or the abused may refuse to allow visits or calls from other siblings or professionals or well-meaning neighbors. Thus the destructive actions remain hidden. Alternatively, where an elderly person refuses visits from a child or a sibling, it might be a signal that the elderly person considers the relative to be destructive, negative, or untrustworthy.

Exploitation

Exploitation includes scams, stealing money, identity theft, and people posing as grandchildren to get money for emergencies or threatening predicaments. The exploited fall victim to telephone and e-mail requests to give their account numbers, social security numbers, and vital information. Under the guise of needing to update accounts, swindlers collect information for their theft. The elderly and vulnerable need to be aware that there are robot callers who dial at random until someone answers; then the swindler asks questions that lead to verifying a relative's (usually a grandchild's) name, eligibility, or account. Also, there are crank e-mails aimed at getting bank information such as check and routing numbers.

Investment scams include Ponzi schemes, promissory notes, unscrupulous financial advisors, and inappropriate or fraudulent annuity sales. And *affinity fraud* targets people who have connections to the military or have a particular religious affiliation or ethnic identity.

People are "vulnerable to erroneous claims and vulnerable due to grief from loss of spouse, family member, friend, or pet."[100] They may "be lonely and socially isolated." They tend to "be trusting and polite."[101] They should never gauge another person's trustworthiness by sound of voice, smooth talking, or a supposedly legal letter (erroneous with lies). People are encouraged to check for suspicious charges or incorrect information on Medicare summary notices or explanations of benefits. As a federal agency has advised, "Beware of offers of free medical equipment, services or goods in exchange for your Medicare number."[102]

The vulnerable are unaware of the schemes with which they are victimized. They want to be cooperative and they act without checking the legitimacy of those seeking their help. To combat the con artist, they can simply question and remember how can they win a prize, etc., if they had not entered in the first place. They can be wary when the telephone conversation

---

[100] Ibid., 5.

[101] Ibid.

[102] Ibid., 26.

begins with "This is not a sales call." They should be wary of pressure to make a decision or give information in response to a fast-talking sales pitch. They can remember that one's bank or credit union will not ask for information, since it already has it. Other warning signs should apply to "lump sum payment arrangements (equivalent of a 60–70 percent annual interest rate) and arrangements that allow creditors to access the account where you receive your benefits."[103]

Elderly and others fall victim to fraudulent claims because they forget that there is no free lunch and that if something sounds too good to be true, it is. Also there are those so desperate for money or help that they grab at anything.

Many elderly have pride and want independence. Therefore, they do not report it when they are victimized. Or they don't adequately seek information before cooperating with a requestor. They are impatient and do not take another day to decide about participation. If they would ask for the name of the organization and the caller's name and telephone number, the perpetrator will probably hang up, thus verifying it as a scam or crime.

---

[103] Ibid., 38.

The Federal Deposit Insurance Corporation (FDIC) reports that exploitation is a crime. Older Americans lost over $2.9 billion from it.[104] In addition to risks from the broad spectrum of perpetrators, there can be "mild cognitive impairment" that diminishes the elder person's "ability to make sound financial decisions." And once swindled, the elderly have little opportunity to regain what they lost, which may limit ability to live independently and lead to other adverse effects such as "decline in health, broken trust, and fractured families." Reporting and early intervention are imperative.

Another type of exploitation is when a person is dependent on a family member, a caregiver, a minister, a representative of an institution, or someone else who pressures them for money or control of their finances. Theft of money or property is often accomplished by a caregiver or in-home helper.

Other traps are lottery and sweepstake scams, telemarketer scams, computer and Internet scams, reverse mortgage fraud, and contractor or home improvement scams.

---

[104] Ibid.

Older adults don't report exploitation and abuse because of self-blame; they think they deserve or caused the abuse. In addition to shame and embarrassment, some victims fear retaliation. They fear they will not be believed or will lose their independence by being considered incompetent and thus will be moved into that dreaded place called a "nursing home."

"A durable power of attorney is a very important tool in financial incapacity due to Alzheimer's disease, another form of dementia, or other health problems."[105] Consult an attorney regarding a power of attorney document, a trust, or some other legal document that turns over authority to a reliable intercessor.

Mobilizing Resources

Resources include community and government services, hospital social services, family members or extended family, and faith-based services. Knowledge itself is another resource, as is faith in one's self and the Creator. Mobilizing resources in the community requires awareness of those resources, contact information, personal management skills, and courage to

---

[105] Ibid., 10.

act upon knowledge or leads that one gets from others. There are food markets, pantries, health clinics, and government assistance such as Meals on Wheels, Homemaker Home Health Services, visiting community nurses, legal aid, legal services, the attorney general, supplemental income benefits, the earned income credit for taxes, neighborhood watch programs, and medical alert pendants to wear at all times. Some type of government adult protective services office is in every state, as are supportive organizations known as area agencies (councils) on aging. Call 1-800-677-1116 or write http://www.eldercare.gov for contacts in your county and in the state department of social services. Check out a broker or investment advisor by logging into http://www.finra.org or calling a consumer hotline at 1-800-289-9999.

Some elders refuse to go to a nursing home because they want to keep their car or truck. They want to maintain their independence. They want to keep their assets and pass down the proceeds of the sale of their home, even if meager, to their child. They say that is all they can give to them. False pride may prevent them from wearing a medical alert pendant such as the one from Lifeline. Touching the pendant puts them in contact with those on a list. If they do not use their phone during the day, the hospital social service worker will call them. The sheriff or police will break in the door to check if no one responds.

Those being abused may need to call the police or protective services. Prosecutors cannot prosecute without a police report or call. But those with dementia or health limitations are unable to take the witness stand. A person may need to be removed from the abusive situation to a better, safer place. It is sometimes difficult to document the actions of abusers. Witnesses are required to document a crime. Nevertheless, certain employees of government or those in the helping professions are required by law to report cases of abuse.

Who Can Help

The Good Samaritan story is the model for us to help strangers who have been abused in various ways. (See Luke 10:31–35.) Jesus used this illustration to identify who is our neighbor after saying the most important commandments are to love God and treat our neighbors as we treat ourselves. We can mobilize resources for vulnerable people in our community, regardless of how well we know them. We can check on them. One model for church ministry shows young church persons going from house to house, asking, "What can we do to help you today?" or "What would you like us to pray about for you today?" Church members could circle on a map their "circle of love," identifying those persons to care for in their neighborhood. This could help to discover those in captivity.

Inspiration to assist others is found in Scripture. Isaiah 61:1 says, "The spirit of the Lord God is upon me, because the Lord has anointed me; he has sent me to bring good news to the oppressed, to bind up the brokenhearted, to proclaim liberty to the captives, and release to the prisoners." And Luke 4:17–19 shows Jesus saying "The Spirit of the Lord is upon me, because he has anointed me to bring good news to the poor. He has sent me to proclaim release to the captives and recovery of sight to the blind, to let the oppressed go free …"

Regular service workers should and do notice irregularities and have someone check on their constituents. These regulars may be persons serving "meals on wheels." Or they are mail carriers, who can notice that the newspaper is not picked up or other indicators of a possible health emergency. Other regulars are neighbors in a neighborhood watch program, which can be presented by representatives. The program can include people in the neighborhood checking on each other.

Professional caregivers such as home health aides who watch someone continually are continually under stress themselves. They often must be aware and provide care twenty-four hours a day. They sometimes are maltreated by a client who lies about them and is complaining all the time. A professional told an audience that such caregivers need eight hours or more of relief from their caregiving. Some patients are mean, cruel, and selfish; and sometimes caregivers are mean, cruel, and selfish.

Courage to Combat Abuse and Alleviate Suffering

Change is possible when we focus on courage more than the condition. Only people with a strong personality will make a report that someone is abusing them or abusing someone else. That is why we have Jesus Christ as our Advocate or a strong brother or sister who is our "keeper." In Genesis 4:9–11, we are told of the question "Am I my brother's keeper?" The answer was clear: that we are keepers of each other. In the New Testament, Jesus promised He would send an advocate to assist in times of trial. We will be given the words to say. We simply have to pray for words, actions, wisdom, and courage, regardless of whether we are the victim or the reporter of abuse. In 1 John 2:1, the words are, "My dear children, I write this to you so that you will not sin. But if anybody does sin, we have an advocate with the Father Jesus Christ, the Righteous One." Under modern judicial processes, a court advocate for the abused person is appointed in alleged abuse cases.

The FDIC recommends, "If you or a loved one is a victim of financial exploitation by a fiduciary [or anyone else], take action immediately and make a report to Adult Protective Services or your local enforcement agency."[106]

A woman told an adult protective services official, "I don't know how I had enough courage to talk to you. I have been living in fear for three years. Finally I drummed up enough courage to ask you about changing my power of attorney." The official from the service changed the power of attorney legitimately. The hospital could have helped the woman also. (Some do not know they can change their power of attorney.) The woman had had appointed an unscrupulous power of attorney

---

[106] Ibid.

after locating him on the Internet. He was making all the decisions, and matters became worse and worse. She said she did not know from whom she got the courage. But we know it was from the power of the Holy Spirit.

Psalm 31:1–5 (*NLT*) inspires us.

> O Lord, I have come to you for protection; don't let me be disgraced.
>
> Save me, for you do what is right. Turn your ear to listen to me; rescue me quickly. Be my rock of protection, a fortress where I will be safe. You are my rock and my fortress. For the honor of your name, lead me out of this danger. Pull me from the trap my enemies set for me, for I find protection in you alone. I entrust my spirit into your hand.
>
> Rescue me, Lord, for you are a faithful God.

Rejoice! Spring forth! We are healed! We are renewed!

Part III
Prayer, Praise, and Power

In this part, I present poems I have written about renewal and healing. Reading such poetry assists in spiritual, emotional, and physical change. References to Scripture in the poems validate the themes throughout the book and in the poems themselves. Some poems are prayers. Some have underlying praises. Some bring power to renewing and healing of life issues. Choosing to read one or two poems day by day can provide wisdom and truth, infilling of the Holy Spirit, calmness of the soul, courage, and hope.

Life Renewal

Life was misery and torment.
Evil forces were evident.
Life was a constant trial
For I was in denial.

Life received the blows.
Life lay in shadows.
Life was in despair
Because Christ I didn't know.

Then across the horizon, beauty shone
From the inner wellspring,
From touch of Creator, love of a friend,
Christ lifted me again.

A new spark did ignite;
I heard a song in the night.
Faintly I saw the Light.

I sensed God's mercy and might.
I was wrapped in music
As a new walk I took.
My soul knew revival
And my heart felt tearful.

Jesus knocked and I said, "Enter."
He said, "We need to talk more than ever."
I said, "I surrender to your will"
Even though the ways I knew not still.
Surrendering to God is a move of strength,
For with me the King of Life
Strengthens me in battles and in strife.
I am not always victorious but faithful;
God reigns in my life ever joyful.
Renewed by the Creator's power,
I praise, pray, and sing each hour.
Road is brighter, load lighter, vision clearer.
Recharged with currents from the Great Transformer.

My Heart

My heart creates a melody
Healing the wounds of yesterday.
In my heart there is a new Friend.
The ache of loneliness on the mend,
In my heart an unfinished song
Attempting to wrap up the guilt of my wrong.

In my heart beauty of nature fair
Forgives those whom my heart did tear.
In my heart, the blood flows on,
Filling the vacancy with the Son.

In my heart, the stones people threw
Didn't keep me from life anew.
Where my heart was stabbed,
The Great Physician sews stitches
So I am not too, too sad.

In my heart, now filled with joy,
I love and serve others, too.
My wounded heart is a gift
Of healing balm to help you.

I Lost a Part of Me

I lost a part of me
- A death of a special friend
- A devastating divorce
- Lost employment and purpose
- Loss of a bodily limb

I lost a part of me
- I mourn its existence
- It is here with me constantly
- In the memory of what was
- But never again will be

I lost a part of me
- It is gone forever
- I mourn the lost
- I will never be the same
- I must change or be stuck forever

I lost a part of me
- But I gained humility
- Along with anger

I gained wisdom
Along with incapacity
I lost a part of me
No longer perfectly able
Never was able perfectly
Just limping along
The whole day long
I lost a part of me
But it is easier to repair
Than an inward scar
Than a broken heart
Than trust in one I sought
I lost a part of me
Some say there went my dignity
My pride is that I survived
But those who scorn and sneer
Don't see the beauty inside of me
(Do not see the pain and suffering either)
I lost a part of me
But I gained appreciation
Thankfulness for other parts
Parts working together
In harmony, overlooking the loss

I lost a part of me
- I turn to remaining parts
- Waiting for me to care
- Checking on them for repair
- Thanking them for being a part

I lost a part of me
- Other parts come to the rescue
- My heart is stronger to move
- My mind sharper to work smarter
- Muscles have new avenues

I lost a part of me
- But gained new choices:
- Will the past determine my day or
- Will the future determine my day?
- Let the lost be always lost or
- Keep the lost in bitter memories?

I lost a part of me
- Now I am more than I was
- My heart with more understanding
- My mind with more wisdom
- Strength shifted from another part

I lost a part of me
- But gained connections and more

Connections with others less than whole
Connections with the Great Transformer
Connections with currents through my soul

I lost a part of me
    Then I became disabled
    But I gained creativity
    Power for new mobility
    Operating while missing a part

I lost a part of me
    I turn on the ignition
    Crank up the shaft
    Create some new gas
    My body is going to last

I lost a part of me
    Now, new goals to pursue
    Exploring new possibilities
    Prayer, practice, persistence
    I can also gain a new totality

I lost a part of me
    Getting in touch with my heart
    I've more courage than thought
    Getting in touch with my mind
    More capacity to imagine than taught

I lost a part of me
> While new skills to develop
> New unknown paths to view
> New territories to conquer
> Through valleys to the table (Psalm 23)

I lost a part of me
> Cutting my losses
> Counting blessings one by one
> It surprises me
> What the Lord hath done

I lost a part of me
> Thank you heart, soul, mind, and strength
> You are my life parts making me whole
> Cosmic energy flows through to you
> Your power within surges anew

I lost a part of me
> New functions to behold
> I'm differently abled.
> Rejoice! I'm God abled!

I lost a part of me
> But I gained eternity
> Rejoice! I'm not alone
> Love and power propel me.

Too Busy to Care

I am too busy,
> Sitting on my pity pile,
> Stirring the ashes of my life,
> Recalling errors of yesterday
> And all its strife,
> Feeling past hurts bestowed over the miles,
> Processing traumas accumulated in aisles,
> Too busy licking my wounds,
> Too lonely to notice others crying
> Over dear ones who are dying.

Today I leave the crisis on the shelf a while.
> I take time to sing and pray.
> I look up to the mountain.
> I drink from life's fountain.
> I walk another mile.
> I help others on their way.

Helping others increases my time
And I am renewed as I dine.
I notice someone who is too busy,
Give encouragement, kind words sharing.

I am busy now,
    Sweeping up the pity pile,
    Burying ashes with a smile,
    Having a funeral for my old self,
    Closing page on my old chapter,
    Looking for beautiful new wealth,
    Ignoring the shadows,
    Cooking a new stew,
    Drinking a new wine,
    Listening to a new voice
    As I say "I am Thine."

Now ... I am not too busy—
    Not too busy to know,
    Not too busy to care,
    Not too busy to find
    Those who need me to be loving and kind.

You Are All Right

It's all right to have worry;
    Wisdom comes not in a hurry.
It's all right to have trouble;
    You will get through the muddle.
It's all right to have fright;
    Trust in the Lord's great might.
It's all right to be scared;
    Look upward, forward, anywhere.
It's all right to be disabled;
    You are brave and God abled.
It's all right to have pain;
    You will have peace again.
It's all right to cry and cry;
    God your broken heart repairs.
It's all right to wander away;
    You will come back another day.
It's all right if unable to move;
    Your heartbeat again does prove.

It's all right to have some fear;
> Your own Creator is near.

It's all right to doubt and question;
> Remember you are beautiful—

To God you are His delight! (Zephaniah 3:17)

(This poem was written by request and distributed at the 2011 conference of the Governor's Council for People with Disabilities, in Indiana.)

Pain

Jesus, heal me.
Make me whole.
Restore the spirit
In my soul.

Jesus, take pain
So I can rest
At peace in thee,
Secure in love's nest.
Jesus, my pain
Began but spread
From a physical
To pain mental
And pain social
Buried in emotional.

Or maybe my pain
Began as
Emotional, social
Traveling to mental
Caught in the physical.

I still lie here,
Withered, worn.
Pain encompasses,
Traps and destroys.

God, you said
"Be still and know." (Psalm 46:10; Psalm 37:7; Mark 4:39)
Send your power
To endure and show
Your healing touch.

Jesus, I read (Matthew 4:24)
People brought to you
Those with severe pain need
And you healed them indeed.

I may not be cured
But I can be healed
As you touch
Spiritual, emotional
Submerging physical.

Jesus, I read (Revelation 21:4)
You wipe away tears,
No mourning or pain.
So I trust in you
To destroy my fears.

I am also grateful
For medical personnel
Who manage our pain
With pills and skills.

Cover me with a song. (Zephaniah 3:17)
Let me know your delight,
Feel your arms tight,
Strengthened by thy might.
Jesus, your love,
Now with healing power,
Bathes my pain,
Gives victory this hour. Amen.

Gratitude to Drive the Demons Away

Depression fills our souls
Demons destroy our selves
Despair shadows our walk
Disillusionment gives doubts.

What can give us renewal?
What can give us hope?
What can bring happiness?
What restores peace?

Gratitude destroys the demons
Gratitude lifts us from despair
Gratitude replaces depression
Gratitude brings joy.

So thank the Lord as
We share our burdens
As we begin our petitions
As we cry for help.

Gratitude replaces depression in
Our mind, heart, soul, and strength. Amen!

Thanks Giving Every Day

Thanks giving every day
In what we think, do, and say.

Thanks giving every day
Amidst sorrow, pain, and trials.
Thanks giving every day,
Content in want or plenty. (Philippians 4:12–13)

Thanks giving every day
For Strength internally.

Thanks giving every day
For God's constant care and love.
Thanks giving every day
For power to walk or move.

Thanks giving every day
For making it there on time.

Thanks giving every day
For those smiling on the way.

Thanks giving every day
To start again each new day.

Wake Up

Wake up to the Morning Light.
Be renewed for what you do. (Colossians 3:9–10)
Feel the joy in the morning (Psalm 65:8; 90:14)
After a night of mourning.

Today know what God can do. (Hebrews 2:10; 10:32)
Depression is replaced with gratitude.
See His hand moving through and through;
This proves that God cares for you!

 *Weak Knees*

Weak knees and tired arms. (Hebrews 12:11–15)
We sink in life's alarms.
We fall into the pits
Shaken out of our wits.

Remember friends, "Don't lose heart,"
2 Corinthians 4:16 says,
"Though outwardly we are wasting away,
Inwardly we are being renewed day by day."

Lift up your knees and hands in praise.
Give over your legs with pain.
Accept God's gift—the little white pill.
Take the hand of Jesus, and stand!

Life is in heart, mind, soul, and strength
Where God's love also richly flows.
That is where love to Him resides.
The Spirit gives us comfort and joy
Transcending earthly pain and sorrow.

Garden for My Soul

O, for a garden to nourish my soul,
Designed by the Creator to make me whole,
Replenished daily by the Living Water.
After going through valley of shadows below,
The Gardener pulls the weeds of anxiety
That would hurt, choke, and entangle.

The Great Gardener restores my soul
To receive the blessings, fruits from his table.
He transforms tears from a night of mourning
Into dewfall for joy in the morning.
The Gardener provides Eternal Son light,
Making me alive with forgiveness,
Love, hope, peace, beauty, and might.

Just a Little Son Light

(Many of my plants need just a ray of sunlight each day to bloom or grow well.)

Just a little Son light
Makes us bloom
Makes us well
Stirs our very souls.

We hide in the shadows;
The Son light finds us.
If just a little reaches us
Mercy and goodness follow.

We grope to find our way;
With a little Son light to guide,
We walk through the valley,
We survive the turmoil.

Just a little Son light
Can save us,
Can make us grow;
Jesus, a little we know.

Open a crack in your window,
Open your heart's small door,
Open mind and body for power and might
To receive just a little Son light.

Thank you, Jesus,
For not passing us by,
For giving a ray of hope
In answer to our cry! Amen.

Lesson of the Falling Leaves

(As to rising in our redemption, see Psalm 111:9; 130:7; Romans 3:24; Ephesians 1:7; Colossians 1:14; Proverbs 24:16. The "Christ Cycle" is shown in Luke 2:34; 2 Corinthians 1:9–11; Romans 5:21–6:14; 1 Peter 1:3.)

Leaves fall against the blue sky
Leaves fall toward the green grass.
Leaves fall on the hard cement.

Crackle, groan, falling to die,
New leaves wait for coming spring;
New life waits for time of rebirth.

Likewise we fall when we sin. (John 8:21, 24)
Likewise we fall when we despair. (Luke 2:34)
Likewise we fall in weakness and die.

We wait—the Lord renews our strength. (Isaiah 40:31)
We rise in our redemption.
We rise in our resurrection. (Luke 20:37–38)

Life is reborn again in us. (Titus 3:5; Colossians 3:1)
Spirit power surges within us. (1 Peter 3:18–21)
The Great Transformer changes us.

The lesson of the falling leaves
Has shown us rebirth—the Christ Cycle—
Has shown us renewal: God's ways! (John 12:24)

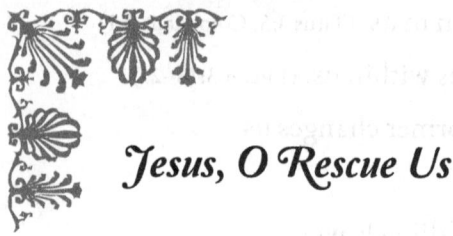

Jesus, O Rescue Us

Jesus, O rescue us
From the terrors of our life.
Jesus, O rescue us
From our pain and strife.

Jesus, O rescue us
So we may see more clearly.

Jesus, O rescue us
So we may love more dearly.

Jesus, O rescue us
So we may serve more fully. (Luke 1:74–75)
Amen.

If We Lose All

What is our pursuit?
Wealth, health, and happiness.

What is our desire?
To love and be loved.

What is our goal?
To get through the day and survive the night.

What is our dream?
To be comfortable and comfort those we love.

What is our mission?
To preserve self and gain new territory.

What if we run the race and lose?
What if we lose all to those beyond our control?
What is left behind?
A still small voice saying, "I am Thine."

After Hope Is Gone

Hope within me dies.
Here in my pain I lie,
Tormented by years past,
Anxious for a future to last.

Numb with cruelties on me bestowed,
Regrets with my mistakes untold,
Tired with work I collapse—
Too weary with having a relapse.

I sink in life's alarms,
Dreading the coming of more harms.
A few hours of sleep
And the thought of asking help
From the Lord escapes.
Still too exhausted to pray,
Words cannot express what to say.
I resign and let the Spirit pray

With sighs beyond words for today. (Romans 8:26–27)
A bit of peace comes my way
For a few moments but not to stay.

A simple warmth replaces the constant dwelling on the past
With the indwelling of the great "I AM" at last.
Crawling in the valley of the shadows, (Psalm 23)
I see faintly the flickering light
Leading to the green meadows.
For an instant, the agonizing worry for the future
Is replaced with the eternal "I AM" to assure.
My heart beats; my blood flows.
My breath comes and goes.
The great "I AM" again speaks.
The Spirit invades my soul.

For a few moments my spirit is renewed.
Love has caught me, held me, uplifted me.
Life again is cautiously pursued.

Savior of Suffering

My heart is wounded and broken.
Rejection from others is unspoken.
My body is torn and twisted with pain;
My mind is angry and disillusioned;
My whole being suffers.
I hear the news about here and abroad;
I mourn for those I know and those in other lands.
Conscience is warped seeing injustice and doing nothing.
I cry out with critical proclamations;
My grieving expands.

The pain of loss is too much to bear:
Loss of children from war, illnesses, accidents, drugs, and disobedience;
Loss of sweetheart love from unfaithfulness, selfishness, and meanness;
Loss of mission from anti forces;
Loss of limb, mind, and capacities.

My body is wounded and broken;
I need replacement parts.
Now I search and move carefully
Just to reposition comfortably,
Thankful for a moment without pain.

I lie in my bed of tears;
I remain numb with many hurts;
I close my eyes to escape reality;
I sink in life's alarms.

I fear the terrors of the night;
I feel the arrows of the day;
I crawl in the valley of shadows;
I stumble searching for light to guide me.

I ask, "Where is the God who cares?"
I cry, "Where is the God upon whom to cast our burdens?"
I pray, "Where is the Lord who reassures?"
I shout, "Where is the Lord who rescues from despair?"
I beg, "How do I get out of this hopeless pit?"

I cease thinking, stop asking, forget praying—
Heart, soul, mind, and strength are too tired
From grieving, too disturbed from confusion, too hopeless to care.
Then I hear a still small voice whisper
"They that wait upon the Lord will renew their strength."
And God meets me in my suffering, face to face.

Weary from mourning, I wait …
"Joy comes in the morning,"
A ray from the Light,
With a faint song in my heart,
With a glimpse of an angel,
With a flickering candle in the dark,
From God came a spark from the Holy Energy
And a slight warmth from the Divine Reality.

I can breathe, although slowly;
I can walk, although feebly;
I can rejoice, although not fully.
God stretched out his hand—
I took it while I was suffering.

Living with Chronics

Operating on five cylinders, not six.
Need a new starter from time to time.
Weak knees, tired arms. (Hebrews 12:11–12)
Limping along all day long.
Need new ways to get around.

A white pill keeps blood pressure down.
A shot of insulin keeps sugar utilized.
Mind over matter for brave souls,
These make life bearable, workable,
With chronic illnesses and disabilities.

Life is a challenge to outwit obstacles.
Life is following doctor's orders.
Life is monitoring signs for success.
Life is finding remedies for ills beset.

We look at vital signs.
We feel the pains.
We try a different approach.
We search for some peace.

The joys of life jump for us.
If we notice, there are delights,
Cherished moments of less pain.
And we give thanks for movement gained.

The gifts of the Spirit to us
Are patience, perseverance,
Smiling while suffering.
We are renewed inwardly not outwardly. (2 Corinthians 4:16)

Live with chronics.
Keep going somehow.
Serve beyond simply going.
Serve the Lord in some way.

At least, for others, pray.
Use any gifts you have, don't delay.
Be proud, be braced, be radiant.
In the Lord, be strong.

Chronics are our cross to bear.
Our hope is to be healed, not cured.
Our life anew is the
Inner strength in me—You.

Our mind in Christ
Makes our body better.
Christ in our soul
Makes us whole.

Living with our Christ
While having chronics
Renews mind and spirit,
Glowing as his light is lit.

Silent Prayer

Sit, kneel, or stand.
This is God's time
Not in formal rhymes.
Neither spoken nor planned,
What God brings to mind
Is the agenda, not mine.
Focus on God, I pray,
But my mind wanders.
That is now okay;
God follows the way.

My thoughts ramble
And some go astray.
Fears and worries arise;
I ask God to speed their demise.
Names of those I love
Come for God to bless.
Names of those I hate

Come for God to shake.
What, God do I feel?
What, God do I do?
I am weak without you.
I am weary all day through.
I listen to his response;
It is fuzzy to hear,
Hard to remember,
Since I am stuck on myself.

A voice says, "Be still."
A whisper is heard,
His presence more real.
In silent prayer he abides.
I look into his face
When in prayer I come,
Reminded of all my sin
And the need for repair.

Forgive me, I plead.
Help me forgive others
And remember those in need.
But I focus on me instead.

I moan, I groan, I sigh.
My heart, mind, and soul do open.
God looks intensely inside.
His Presence has spoken.

Still my mind wanders away
To earthly cares and passions:
Did I turn the fire down low?
Did I lock the doors?
Where is my daughter?
What's happening at the office?
Should I buy the car today?
What will my relatives say?

My silent prayer rescues me
From confused thoughts stirring,
From evil thoughts alarming,
From fearful thoughts anxiety filling,
From depressing thoughts stifling.

Communing with my Creator
In silent prayer with only
The two of us together,
Love has been renewed forever.

I rise from silent prayer
Thinking more clearly,
Loving more dearly,
Having hope more lively.
For silent prayer has been
A moment for eternity.

Cleaning House

Today I clean house.
As I work, I pray.
Having my hands in the sink
Frees my mind to think.

It is a joy to clean.
Things become more bright,
More sparkly, bring delight.
I appear as a queen.

I wash the dirt from
Floors, stools, and sidewalks,
Pick burrs that dragged me down,
Flush down garbage, bad talks.

I shine a light on walls.
I wipe away old dust,
Remove olden pains,
Feel new life in veins.

I sweep trash out the door,
Cleaning the debris,
Replacing with new habits,
Not taking seven demons more. (Luke 11:24–26)

Cleaning the house of my heart
Is a weekly chore
To freshen soul and mind
And renew me evermore.

Walking with Jesus

Jesus gently knocks on your door.
You invite him to enter in.
Jesus asks you to take a walk with him.
You ponder if you can.

No, you say, I must stay;
I have too many children today;
I have to hurry to the office and then play;
No, I won't walk; I will just pray.

Jesus smiles and says,
>I understand—
>I'll come back when you cannot stand.
>I will offer my hand.
>We will walk all over the land.
>We will walk the city streets,
>And perhaps a beggar we will meet,
>Or a lonely person to greet.

We will add your children to your side.
They too will abide
With stronger shoes and feet,
With wisdom and faith to guide.

We will go to the office as you did before,
But with new courage and vision to explore.
We will visit the sick, the poor,
And those imprisoned near your door.

We will go through the wilderness.
We will go through the valley of shadows
But come out refreshed, stronger, and
Seeing more clearly than before.

We will walk amidst the traffic and know the way.
We will see the guiding Light in the night.
We will climb the mountainside,
For hand in hand with the Father we abide.

Walking with Jesus in all that we do,
The path becomes smoother, our shoes become stronger.
The burdens become lighter.
The joy in serving others shines through.

Moving Along—
The New Year

Moving along—
All the day long,
Spurred by New Year's dawning,
Spawned by new life's coming.
These are the gifts to go!

Moving along—
From last year's suffering,
After last year's darkening;
The Light newly beckons on.
These are the gifts to know!

Moving along—
With a new song,
The Light newly guides on,
With visions alluring.
These are the gifts to behold!

Moving along—
With eyes to seek new missions,
With ears to hear new callings,
With hands to provide service.
These are the gifts to show!

Moving along—
Marching in step with the Drum of Life;
The heart beats to end strife;
The mind thinks better thoughts:
Strength to build new temples!
Moving along—
New life in my veins,
New hope in my soul,
Courage to conquer fears,
Grace to cover mistakes.
These are New Year's gifts to take!

Lead Me to Victory

Lead me to success in the eyes of God;
As I pray in the day, the Spirit leads each step.

To not falter in the way
To avoid temptation of evil's sway
To walk in God's reign, not the crowd.

To chase enemies to make them friends
To give hope, restoring beauty from ashes
To see the gifts in every one.

To correct my errors and make amends
To swallow cruel words and mean insults
To ask forgiveness of those and of God.

To survive the stones and arrows
To have peace amid pain and sorrow
To have strength for God's work to do

To encourage sisters and brothers
To deny self in serving others
To help another in the pathway.

To pursue healthy avenues
To destroy bad habits that drag on
To not give up until the battle is won.

To go through the valley of the shadows
To reach the blessings from the table
To know assurance from trusting as able.
Lead me to victory remembering Calvary,
Where upon the cross, Jesus paid the price for me.
Lead me to victory, remembering the resurrection;
I too can have life anew, a new creation.
Lead me to thanks and praise, and action. Amen.

A Moment in Eternity

This hour I breathe a moment in eternity
Not burdened with guilts of yesterday
Not anxious for fears of tomorrow—
The Great "I AM" has appeared to me. (Exodus 3:13–16)

I bathe in the river of Love.
The warmth of the Son shines through.
The sky appears even more blue.
My spirit feels joy anew.
A song vibrates in my heart,
Giving a message, a new start.

Power surges through my soul.
Peace settles my frazzled nerves.
Physically, not all cured,
Spiritually healed, made whole.

My burdens lifted for a while
By the caring Great Shepherd.
The Spirit Counselor in me
Examines them to know how to solve.

I hear the still whisper of God
As I stand on the cliff and wait—
Trust in the faithful Lord, I pray.
Heaven is again within me now
At this time in my life's journey.

Conclusion:
The Key to Continued Renewal

Rescue, encouragement, power, hope, and healing are possible from applying the principles of this book, *Springing Forth*. No matter what the loss, illness, affliction, or aging, we can be renewed. Day by day we can gain strength and joy from practicing the messages. They are new and unique; they can be personalized. Read and do the practical steps daily, or monthly as a reminder. Step 30, in particular, combines a change in perspectives with promises and hope for the future. Equipping us for the steps are the Scriptures and songs in this book, *Springing Forth*.

The essays are from people who have experienced renewal. Their messages demonstrate that mental, technical, social, and spiritual actions are all required if a person is to change and grow from afflictions and losses.

The poems, when read and individualized, help one internalize the themes throughout the book *Springing Forth*. They offer laments, praise, spiritual introspection, and hope.

We can pray as follows:

> Almighty God and Father, we adore You from all life has come and to Whom all life returns! Give to those who are suffering under the burden of years hope and joy. Fill them with gratitude for their many years and make them rich in love. As they grow older on the outside make them younger on the inside through the work of the Holy Spirit. Use this to prepare them, Lord, for the joys of eternal life. Amen.[107]

---

[107] Fr. Joseph Mary Wolfe, MFVA, *EWTN Family Prayer*, B4. Copyright © 2011, EWTN Catholic Publishing, 5817 Old Leads Road, Irondale, AL 35210. Included by permission. Father Wolfe is a member of the Missionaries of the Eternal Word and currently serves as chaplain of the Eternal Word Television Network.

We can sing or make music as well as pray the following prayer:

> Holy Spirit, Lord of Light, from the clear celestial height, Thy pure beaming radiance give! Heal our wounds, our strength renew! On our dryness pour Thy dew! Wash the stains of guilt away! Bend the stubborn heart and will, melt the frozen, warm the chill, guide the steps that go astray! Give us comfort when we die, give us life with Thee on high, give us joys that never end! Come O Holy Spirit, come![108]

Amen.

---

[108] Wolfe, *EWTN Family Prayer*, B18.

Other Books by the Author

The Shepherd's Guide through the Valley of Debt and Financial Change: **A Comprehensive Manual for Financial Management, Counseling, & Spiritual Guidance.** (AuthorHouse. ISBN 978-1-4490-0572-6) Pastoral care and counseling. Crisis Management. Financial Literacy. 2009, 2015. **Order from AuthorHouse** 888-280-7715 ($27.00) or www.authorhouse.com (Click on bookstore, type The Shepherd's Guide) $27.00 or write 1663 Liberty Drive, Suite 200, Bloomington, IN 47473 or **order from Flora Williams, $21.60,** (includes postage/handling) 3815 Gate Road, Lafayette, IN 47909 (20% discount). florawill@aol.com 765-474-4232 (two or more @ $20).

Financial Literacy at Life Stages: Budgeting, Credit, Funding College, Retirement, Responses to Crises. **A Family Resource Management Manual.** Goals, Decisions by Stages of Life, Earning, Spending, Response to Financial Crises. 2012. **Order from author Flora Williams.** $16.50 or $15.00 for quantity. 765-474-4232, florawill@aol.com, 3815 Gate Road, Lafayette, IN 47909.

Renewal: A Collection of Flora's Poetry
(Arolf Publisher, 2013)
Overcoming disability, living with loss, handling chronic illnesses and pain are featured. Messages through ninety-eight poems are life changing and thought provoking. They give hope, renewal, inspiration, and courage. Scripture is referenced. Poems are ideal for use in worship services, meetings, meal-time conversations, and personal devotions. Author Rev. Dr. Williams graduated from Manchester University, Purdue University, and Bethany Theological Seminary. **Order from author.** $9.50 (includes postage) 765-474-4232 florawill@aol.com. 3815 Gate Road, Lafayette, IN 47909.

Hand in Hand with God: Witnessing on the Way
(Publish America)
Author describes stages of grief after a tragic accident in Mexico leaving her disabled—now God-abled. More than sharing her faith journey and miracles, themes are techniques for witnessing, education for making changes, and overcoming disability. **Order from author Flora Williams.** $10.50 (includes postage) 765-474-4232, florawill@aol.com, 3815 Gate Road, Lafayette, IN 47909.